WINGS No.7

US Air Force Nose Art - Into the '90s

Robert F.Dorr & Norman E.Taylor

Windrow & Greene

Published in Great Britain 1993 by
Windrow & Greene Ltd.
5 Gerrard Street
London W1V 7LJ

A CIP catalogue record for this book is available from the British Library.

ISBN 1-872004-78-4

Published in the USA by
Specialty Press Publishers
& Wholesalers Inc.
PO Box 338
Stillwater, MN 55082
(612) 430-2210/800-888-9653

(Title page) Shark's teeth have been seen on many USAF warplanes over the years. Only the A-10 Warthogs of the 23rd Wing at Pope AFB, North Carolina, can trace their lineage directly to the AVG, the original "Flying Tigers" of World War II. The effect is enhanced by the covers for the A-10's rear-mounted turbofans. *(Norman Taylor)*

Authors' note:

In the captions on these pages, US Air Force terminology consistent with the date of the photo is used. At the beginning of the decade the Air Force had, for instance, Tactical Fighter Wings; most of these became simply Fighter Wings in the recent dramatic reorganization program. The term used with any particular picture must be understood in the context of the date the photo was taken.

Acknowledgements:

Any mistakes in this volume are the responsibility of the authors. This book would have been impossible, however, without the generosity of many others. The authors would like to extend their thanks to Gordon Beem, Ingrid Beuter, Joe Buebe, Bob Bush, Karl Dittmer, MSgt Kevin Foy, Rene J.Francillon, Jerry Geer, MSgt Mike Hrivnak, SSgt Paul Hunt, Craig Kaston, Bob Leavitt, Donald S.McGarry, David W.Menard, SSgt Brandon Middleton, Curvin Miller, Douglas Olson, Major Brian C.Rogers, and the Gang at Roy's. The views expressed in this book are those of the authors and do not necessarily reflect those of the United States Air Force.

Robert F.Dorr
Norman E.Taylor

Nose Art: The Battle Continues...

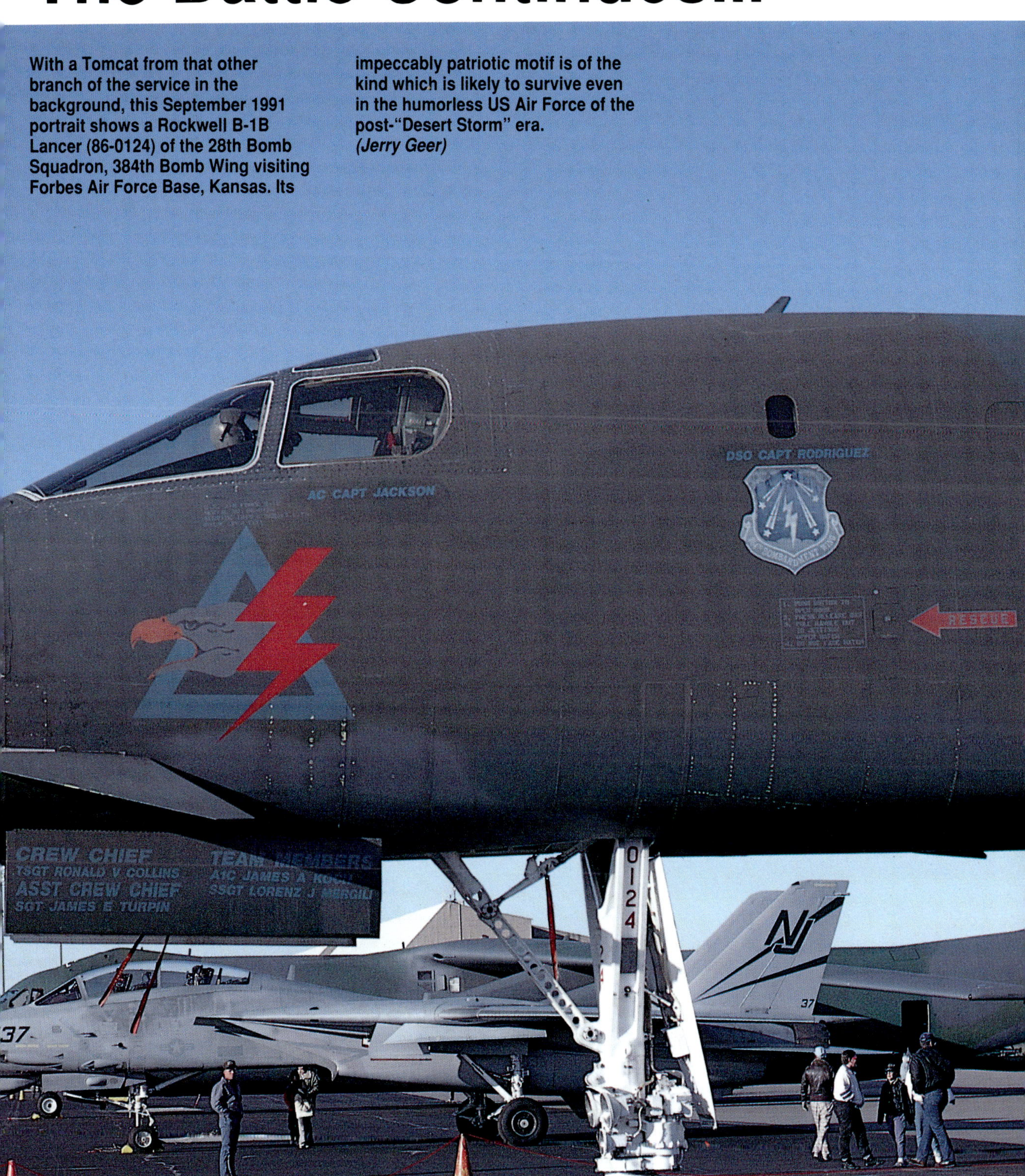

With a Tomcat from that other branch of the service in the background, this September 1991 portrait shows a Rockwell B-1B Lancer (86-0124) of the 28th Bomb Squadron, 384th Bomb Wing visiting Forbes Air Force Base, Kansas. Its impeccably patriotic motif is of the kind which is likely to survive even in the humorless US Air Force of the post-"Desert Storm" era. *(Jerry Geer)*

In mid-1992 the United States Air Force put the final touches to its most dramatic program of change in half a century - indeed, in many respects its most fundamental changes ever.

The USAF slashed the number of its planes and its people. Combat strength fell to the lowest point since the late 1940s, while leaders proclaimed the goal of creating a "lean, mean" expeditionary force for rapid deployment overseas. More importantly, the USAF changed almost every aspect of its operations, its flying, and its preparedness to wage aerial warfare. It even changed its uniform. Gone in an instant was nearly half a century of tradition founded in those twin mainstays of the USAF's fighting force during the Cold War: Tactical Air Command and Strategic Air Command.

It was an unprecedented metamorphosis. Only a year earlier USAF warplanes had come home from the Persian Gulf festooned with bright and gutsy artwork commemorating a decisive victory in Operation "Desert Storm". Now the production lines which turned out those warplanes were beginning to shut down, and the future of the F-15 and F-16 fighters was doubtful. Airmen supposedly in mid-career faced the loss of their jobs as personnel numbers were whittled down. The process began before President Clinton took office, but a further wave of force reductions followed the new Chief Executive's swearing-in on 20 January 1993. By Inauguration Day nose art on aircraft was harder to find, as was the unquestioning confidence and fighting spirit which it echoed, and which had so recently won a war. A broad range of problems gnawed at morale in the service.

The Top Brass were making tough decisions on big issues, and unpopular decisions on small ones. Way down near the bottom of the "trivial" category (at least, to a man in uniform about to lose his job) came the question of how, when and whether airmen would be allowed to reflect their pride in unit, mission and service by using paintbrush, spray can or grease pencil to individualize their warplanes with nicknames, cartoons and slogans.

Few men in Air Force history have been as controversial as Chief of Staff General Merrill A.McPeak. He wrought unprecedented organizational changes; at the other end of the scale he also introduced the unwanted new uniform - and was widely reported to have dressed-down a squadron commander for allowing nose art on a jet fighter. McPeak was behind the three new commands which emerged in mid-1992: Air Combat-

Command (ACC), headquartered at Langley AFB, Virginia; Air Mobility Command (AMC), at Scott AFB, Illinois; and Air Force Materiel Command (AFMC), at Wright-Patterson AFB, Ohio. For his reshaping and redirecting of a much-shrunken air force McPeak was deemed a visionary by many; but was unable to escape the displeasure of those in the ranks who blamed him (often unfairly) for what seemed a reduction not merely in numbers but also in the camaraderie so essential for men and women charged with employing force of arms in defense of freedom. Symbolic of the pinching not only of numbers but also of the human qualities special to the Air Force was an order allegedly sent from McPeak's office to the newly-formed Air Mobility Command, on the subject of its KC-10 and KC-135 tanker aircraft: "I want all nose art removed from those tankers by the first of June (1992)". Just a year earlier nose art, bright colors, flags, yellow ribbons - all the trappings of the military spirit - had blossomed everywhere as Air Force people kicked off the decade with their triumph in "Desert Storm". Artwork broke out like a cheerful rash on just about every type of aircraft - even, as rarely allowed in peacetime, on fighters. Airborne caricature reached dramatic new heights of expression.

Some of it was felt to be getting out of hand. Not everyone appreciated, for example, the reference made to a rooster through the artistry of Staff Sergeant Warren Trask II of the 363rd Tactical Fighter Wing, who christened an F-16C Fighting Falcon *Hot Cock*. Obviously, Trask's rendition of a contented rooster attended by bathing beauties was simply a word-play on the "Fighting Gamecocks" nickname of the 363rd Wing's 19th Squadron. What Trask realized, if General McPeak did not, was that nose art helps morale, unit cohesion and fighting spirit.

The "Old Masters"

It has been said that as soon as military aircraft were invented, high-ranking officers had to be appointed to prevent pesky, free-spirited individuals from adorning them with individual markings. Like the battle banners and military heraldry of old, nose art is used by flyers (and their squires, the crew chiefs) to convey a message to the world.

Artwork on warplanes saw its fullest flowering during World War II. It was not unusual for the nose of a fighter or bomber to bear a caricature of the pilot's wife; or a George Petty or Alberto Vargas nude of a lady who clearly wasn't anybody's wife (at least,

The US Air Force traces its lineage to the US Army Air Corps which, in the golden era between the World Wars, offered unprecedented opportunities to paintbrush virtuosos. This Boeing P-12E biplane fighter (31-559) displays the eye-grabbing variety of colors typical of the 1930s; the propeller and death's-head on an orange disc identify B Flight of the 6th Pursuit Squadron, based at Wheeler Field, Hawaii. The diagonal red stripe on the rear fuselage, when viewed from directly above, formed a perfect "V" behind the cockpit and was used as a spatial reference during formation flying. Although the colors were kaleidoscopic, the female form, cartoon animals, and other popular icons were not commonly painted on warplanes until after Pearl Harbor. ***(David W.Menard)***

not yet...). The most ambitious example ever was probably the 5th Air Force B-24J Liberator in the Southwest Pacific whose nose bore a scantily clad young woman in the clutches of a gloating dragon whose scaly green tail extended over the bomber's entire rear fuselage, inspiring the *double entendre* nickname *The Dragon and His Tail.*

Pre-VJ Day aircraft art echoed the basic preoccupations of fighting men: superstition - in the form of every type of good luck charm; aggressive patriotism - manifesting itself in warlike images of every kind; and the opposite sex. In a 1943 article for the GI newpaper *Stars and Stripes* Andrew A.Rooney - better known today as the curmudgeon of the CBS News broadcast *Sixty Minutes* - could make little sense of it. The enemy "must wonder what the hell kind of air force they are up against", he pondered. "They come diving in, teeth clenched, hell bent for Hitler, and along with a hail of lead they are greeted by the stupid grin of some absurd comic book character, or the nude form of a Petty girl painted on the nose of the bomber they are attacking...."

Nudes, slogans and the buzzwords of contemporary popular culture survived the disapproving glare of the Top Brass during the air wars over Korea in the 1950s and Vietnam in the 1960s. In Korea future astronaut John Glenn got away with painting *MiG Mad Marine* on the F-86 Sabre he flew during an exchange tour with the Air Force; while Perrin Gower had *Terrible Turtle* on his Sabre, an appellation he insists did not refer to a girlfriend. To ease the concerns of a strait-laced commander a B-29 Superfortress named *My Assis Dragon* acquired a wide splotch of paint in the middle to become simply *My...Dragon.* In Vietnam the nickname of the 25th Fighter Squadron was resurrected on an F-4 Phantom entitled *My Assam Dragon.*

We Are Not Amused...

In the 1990s the new Air Force seemed to have real difficulty grasping the evidence from past wars that aircraft nose art might boost *esprit de corps.* The newly formed Air Combat Command seemed even more determined than Air Mobility Command to cut it out. "We've been ordered to do this", admitted Captain Michael P.Curphey in October 1992 when the 416th Wing at Griffiss AFB, New York, ignored the option of toning down its nose art and chose instead to eliminate it altogether from their B-52 Stratofortresses and KC-135 Stratotankers. Gone forever now are *Monkey Business* with its chimp, and *Big Stick* with its club-wielding caveman. "We also had to get rid of mission markings - bombs, palm trees and camels."

It is hard not to sympathize with the plight of the 95th Reconnaissance Squadron, the "Kickin' Asses", equipped with the Lockheed U-2R and stationed at Beale AFB, California. The 95th had as its squadron emblem a provocative image often called "the constipated donkey" or "the donkey at the proctologist's". In 1991 members of the squadron created a new emblem retaining the donkey tradition in a more tasteful manner, consistent with latter-day Air Force preoccupations. It was disapproved by McPeak's staff because they wanted to keep the original version for tradition's sake. A year later orders came down against displaying the donkey. Some days, you just can't win.

Bucking the trend, however, are many icons which can still be found today on ACC warplanes, proclaiming the individual spirit of Air Force people. Even at Griffiss commemorative nose art was retained on B-52s and KC-135s to mark the base's 50th anniversary. Elsewhere in ACC some nose art survives; and many examples persist of stylized unit insignia, tail codes, squadron colors and other outlets for artistry.

When the 2nd Wing at Barksdale AFB, Louisiana, wiped the "Desert Storm" caricatures off its KC-10s, KC-135s and B-52s it retained patriotic artwork, including that identifying one B-52 as *Memphis Belle III.* The historical link with the celebrated B-17F Flying Fortress of the 324th Bomb Squadron, 9lst Bomb Group which starred in William Wyler's 1944 documentary gives such "politically correct" nose art a good chance of surviving even this strait-laced decade. Even obscure nicknames will probably escape the purge of the mid-'90s if they have bona fide historical credentials - like the Air National Guard RF-4C Phantom named *Starize* that still sports nose art originally painted on a World War II bomber.

As if the Top Brass's purse-lipped attitude were not discouraging enough, even the deteriorating standard of education in the USA has been blamed by some for the nasal blandness of the mid-1990s warplane. The prestigious *Air Force Times* quotes Barksdale's MSgt Ron Mullan as lamenting that "right now we don't have any artists talented enough to paint nose art...a guy who did a lot of the nose art at Barksdale has since moved on. But if a crew chief wants to request it, he can."

ACC's former Strategic Air Command bombers and tankers have gained two-letter tail codes, but have lost the artwork which once adorned their mighty fins. B-52s at Griffiss wore a distinctive Statue of Liberty, for example; and those at Carswell AFB, Texas, wore a likeness of the Lone Star State's flag. Both began to disappear in mid-1992.

Those tactical unit identifiers - two-letter tail codes - are actually proliferating in the 1990s. The system is recent in terms of Air Force heritage; it was born in 1966 and extensively modified in 1977. Usually a kind of geographic logic governs the choice of code - EG for Eglin, or LN for Lakenheath, for example - but the paired letters do not always identify a location. (The newly-formed 23rd Wing at Pope AFB, North Carolina has a new FT tail code; depending upon

Shoot You're Covered was a Consolidated B-24J Liberator (44-441750), an example of the most numerous American warplane ever built. On 20 June 1941 the US Army Air Corps was renamed US Army Air Forces; soon afterwards America entered World War II, and irreverent nose art - much of it spicier than this mild word-play on a crap-shooting expression - appeared over every battlefront. During that war, as in all wars, there was a minimum of fuss about perfectly sane men painting immature caricatures on their flying machines if it made them happier. *(Robert F.Dorr)*

whom you ask, this denotes either the 23rd's link to the wartime "Flying Tigers", or the nearby town of Fayetteville.) With the creation of ACC out of the ashes of SAC and TAC, many aircraft types which never before wore tail codes now have them, including B-52s.

Should art appear on the tail of an aircraft? No issue more sharply illustrates the difference in policy between Air Combat Command and Air Mobility Command. Just when ACC decreed that Griffiss's Lady Liberty would have to go - and indeed, that no art at all would be permitted on tails - AMC began to decorate the previously bare vertical fins of its transports. Adopting a practice which had begun in the tanker community, AMC authorized in 1992 colorful tail bands enclosing distinctive symbols for its C-130s, C-141s and C-5s. Typical is the 437th Airlift Wing at Charleston AFB, South Carolina, whose C-141B Starlifters are spruced up with a yellow tail band enclosing the state's crescent moon and palmetto tree.

Rules, and more rules

ACC's guidelines on nose art, more specific than AMC's, restrict size to "no more than 3 feet by 3 feet". Any artwork must be "representative of the unit or civilian community; be distinctive, symbolic and designed in good taste; not portray a specific weapon system or specific mission; enhance unit pride; *and be gender neutral*" (our italics...). AMC's rules allow nose art to be up to 4 feet high by 3 feet wide on KC-135s and up to 5 feet square on KC-10s. The rules also require a wing commander's approval of a design, and specify that no copyrights be violated. An aircraft transferring from one unit to another can retain its individuality only if the receiving commander approves. Although nudes of either sex, and the nicknames to go with them, are clearly out, names such as *City of San Antonio* (a C-5A Galaxy belonging to the 433rd Airlift Wing at Kelly AFB, Texas) and *Freedom's Best* (a KC-135 Stratotanker at Wurtsmith AFB, Michigan) comply with these restrictive caveats.

Shark's teeth are almost never acceptable to the Top Brass, except for Pope AFB's 23rd Wing, which can legitimately trace its lineage to the American Volunteer Group, the "Flying Tigers" who fought in China with shark-toothed P-40s before America's entry into World War II. When the 23rd became a "composite" wing under McPeak's massive reorganization plan, not only its A-10s but also its C-130 Hercules qualified for the "Jaws" orthodontics.

* * *

On these pages the authors present a sampling of USAF nose art of the 1990s. At the time this book goes to press we are less than half way into the decade, and it is almost impossible to foresee what might happen next in an uncertain and rapidly changing world. Certainly, no one could have foreseen "Desert Storm" a year earlier. While the prospects for nose art look relatively bleak in 1993, it is not impossible that airplanes might brighten up again at short notice as the result of some unexpected development.

By far the best-known nose art applied to American warplanes, and since copied the world over: the shark's teeth first sported by Gen. Claire Chenault's American Volunteer Group (AVG), the fabled "Flying Tigers" who fought in the China-Burma-India theater before regular US forces were committed. While AVG veterans are adamant in insisting that only they are entitled to be called "Flying Tigers", their history, traditions, and some of their people were absorbed by the US 14th Army Air Force's 23rd Fighter Group. The aircraft shown here is a Curtiss P-40N Warhawk (42-105927), a later model than the P-40B/D Tomahawks flown in China by Chenault's pilots. *(Robert F.Dorr)*

Major Thomas B.McGuire Jr, second-ranking American air ace of all time, flew a Lockheed P-38 Lightning named *Pudgy (V)* with the markings shown here, including Japanese naval flags recording his 38 aerial victories. These "kill" markings sometimes appeared in the simpler form of the red Japanese *hinomaru* or "meatball" insignia; and fighter pilots in Europe marked their tally in Iron Crosses or swastikas. In Korea and Vietnam kill markings were usually red stars; in the Persian Gulf, green stars. To the purist these symbols of enemy aircraft downed in combat belong to the particular aircraft which scored the victory, and should not be transferred to another airframe even by the same pilot. In practice a pilot will often take his kill symbols with him to another aircraft, on the theory that the achievement belongs to the man rather than the machine. *(Robert F.Dorr)*

Lieutenant Vernon Richards bores through the skies of the ETO in this North American P- 51D Mustang (44-13357) bearing the prominent nickname *Tika IV* inside a stylized arrow. The row of six swastikas records aerial victories, while partial "Normandy invasion stripes" - broad black and white bands usually under the wings and mid-fuselage - were one of many devices to prevent the good guys from shooting up the good guys. This aerial portrait shows aircraft art and markings typical for late 1944. The "B7" fuselage code was assigned to the 374th Fighter Squadron, 361st Fighter Group. *(USAF)*

Shoo Shoo Shoo Baby took its name from a soothing Phil Moore lullaby of 1943. The aircraft is a Boeing B-17G Flying Fortress (42-32076) with a Vargas-style pin-up on the nose, typifying the way female figures were treated with a kind of saucy sentimentality in the 1940s. The "triangle A" on the fin was the symbol of the 91st Bomb Group; *Baby* belonged to the group's 401st Bomb Squadron, identified by the "LL" code, and the "E" was her individual aircraft code. In one form or another letter codes to identify units have appeared and re-appeared on US Air Force aircraft over the years, the latest twist being today's two-character tail codes. Completed bombing missions are signified here by the line of "hash marks" along the upper nose. *(David W.Menard)*

The postwar years produced some glorious colorschemes for the United States Air Force, as this independent branch of the armed services was re-christened on 18 September 1947. A prominent "buzz number" (FS-626) serves the intended purpose of enabling any disgruntled citizen to report the reckless pilot who beats up his potato field. Colonel C.H.Horton is photographed in a Republic F-84E Thunderjet of the 526th Fighter-Bomber Squadron, 86th Fighter-Bomber Group at Niebeburg, Germany, in 1952. The prominent squadron emblem below the cockpit, commander's stripes at mid-fuselage, and chequer blocks at nose and tail should be enough to catch the eye of any aerial passer-by. *(via David W.Menard)*

(Below) *Ace in the Hole/Deal Me In* is a Boeing B-29A Superfortress (44-61872) with stencil lettering recording not merely the names but also nicknames of a couple of its flight crew, as well as a complete roster of maintenance people. Whatever artistic recognition ground crews receive is usually found on the right side of the aircraft; the left side probably displays a more complete flight crew list, and may have different artwork. Color on the nose wheel door is probably a squadron identifier. B-29s flew from Okinawa to strike targets in North Korea during the 1950-53 war; this Superfortress apparently made an impromptu recovery at K-14 Kimpo Air Base near Seoul in mid-1951 due to minor battle damage. *(Gordon Beem)*

(Right) Korean War transport pilot First Lieutenant Joe Buebe stands by his Douglas C-54 Skymaster. A brilliant map of the Korean peninsula, complete with principal place names and surrounding seas, serves as a backdrop for a cartoon Conestoga wagon - a 19th century mode of transport which performed roughly the same job as the hard-working C-54. The mighty team of mules apparently grew by one for each mission. This kind of nose art would probably be allowed even under today's stringent rules. The aircraft commander and crew chief managed to get their names stencilled beneath the cockpit, but co-pilot Buebe did not. *(Joe Buebe)*

A/C COMMANDER
LT. R.L. SIMPSON
CREW CHIEF
T/SGT. ANDREW HERYLA

Captain Karl Dittmer of the 335th Fighter-Interceptor Squadron, 4th Fighter-Interceptor Wing at Kimpo Air Base, Korea, was handy with an F-86 Sabre (he shot down one MiG-15) and with a paintbrush too. The artistically-inclined Dittmer poses with one of five Sabres which he embellished with nose art for himself and his wingmen. *Wham Bam,* bearing his imaginative rendition of Bugs Bunny, is the F-86A Sabre (49-1272) piloted by First Lieutenant Martin J.Bambrick, who also got one MiG kill in Korea. The war gave the newly independent USAF an opportunity to operate aircraft with a wide variety of colorschemes and artwork.
(Karl Dittmer)

(Right, above) Just back from Vietnam, *Cherry Girl* is a MiG-killer (note the red star), and the bearer of one of the more blatant works of art to appear in that conflict; the nude straddling the refueling receptacle is a good deal raunchier than the painted ladies of World War II and Korea. This Republic F-105D (61-1069) wears standard camouflage paint for the Vietnam era, known as the TO 1-1-4 colorscheme after the technical order which prescribed it. Note the tail code, introduced during the Vietnam War. When this "Thud" was placed on display at Norton AFB, California, the young lady was quickly banished.
(Donald S.McGarry)

(Right) In all the USAF's wars painted female likenesses showed up on aircraft as warriors personalized their metal; but the relationship was usually monogamous. *Marlene, Marian and Nancy* were the trademark for a Korean War F-86 Sabre pilot who must have had a way with the ladies. The aircraft is an F-86E (51-2864) belonging to the 39th Fighter-Interceptor Squadron, 51st Fighter-Interceptor Group at Suwon Air Base, Korea. Though not visible here this Sabre also bore two red stars to signify MiG kills.
(Curvin Miller)

RU

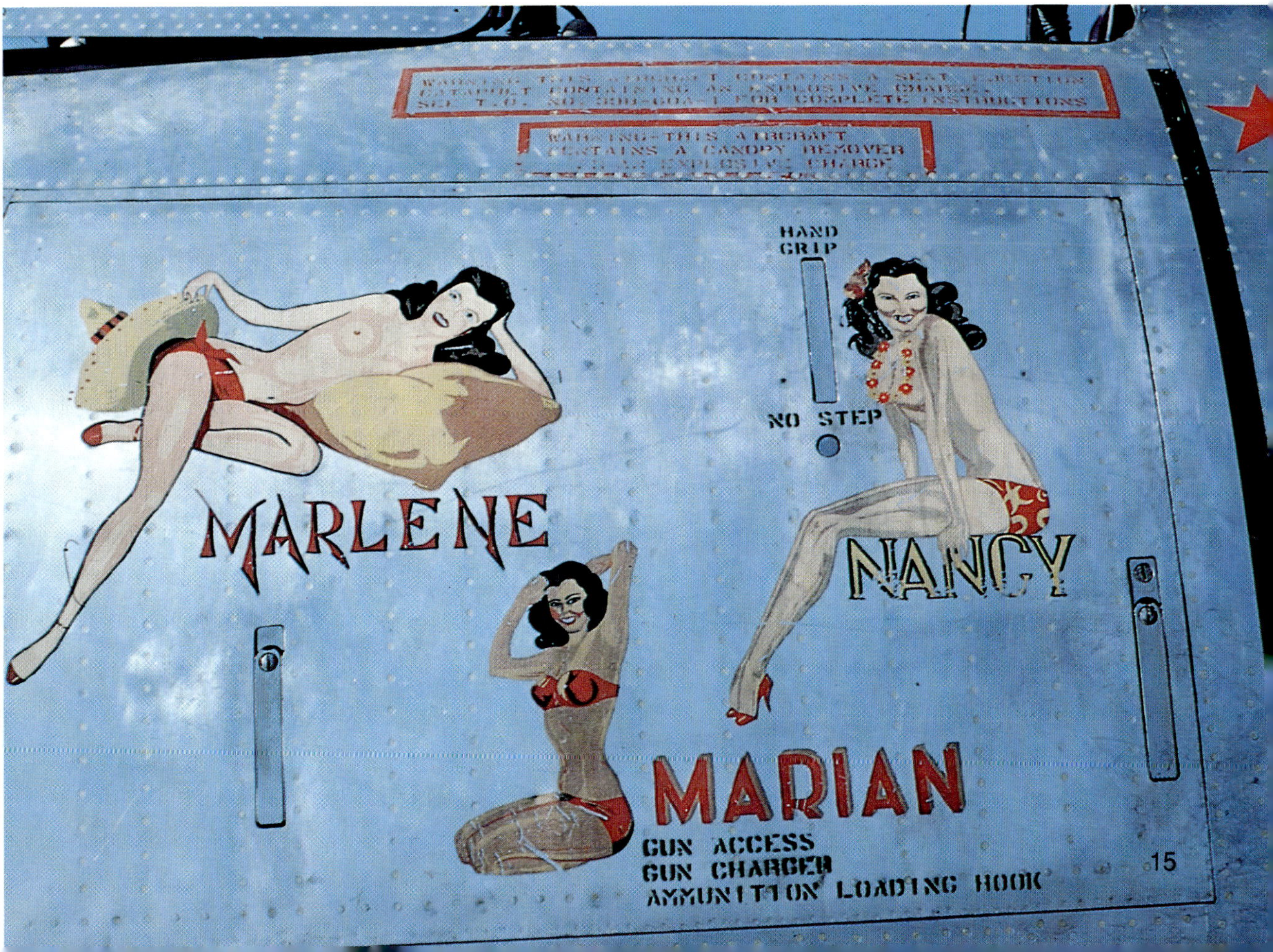
HAND
GRIP
NO STEP
MARLENE
NANCY
MARIAN
GUN ACCESS
GUN CHARGER
AMMUNITION LOADING HOOK

A is for Attack

The Air National Guard, which has both a state and a federal function as part of the US Air Force community, is retiring its fleet of Vought A-7 Corsair IIs; the last should be off the inventory by 1994. This A-7K (80-0288) of the 149th Tactical Fighter Squadron, Virginia ANG, based near Richmond has since been replaced by the F-16C Fighting Falcon. On 24 July 1992 Virginia Governor L.Douglas Wilder ordered the removal of the Confederate flag from all Virginia ANG aircraft after the Richmond *Free-Press* quoted a black Air Guardsman as complaining that racism in the Guard "seems to be sneaking back again" after a period of improved race relations. According to Major Stewart MacInnis of the Virginia ANG, the now-defunct flag was intended "not to imply racism or hatred (but) to symbolize the warrior spirit" of the state's airmen. Aircraft at Richmond still bear individual nicknames. *(Craig Kaston)*

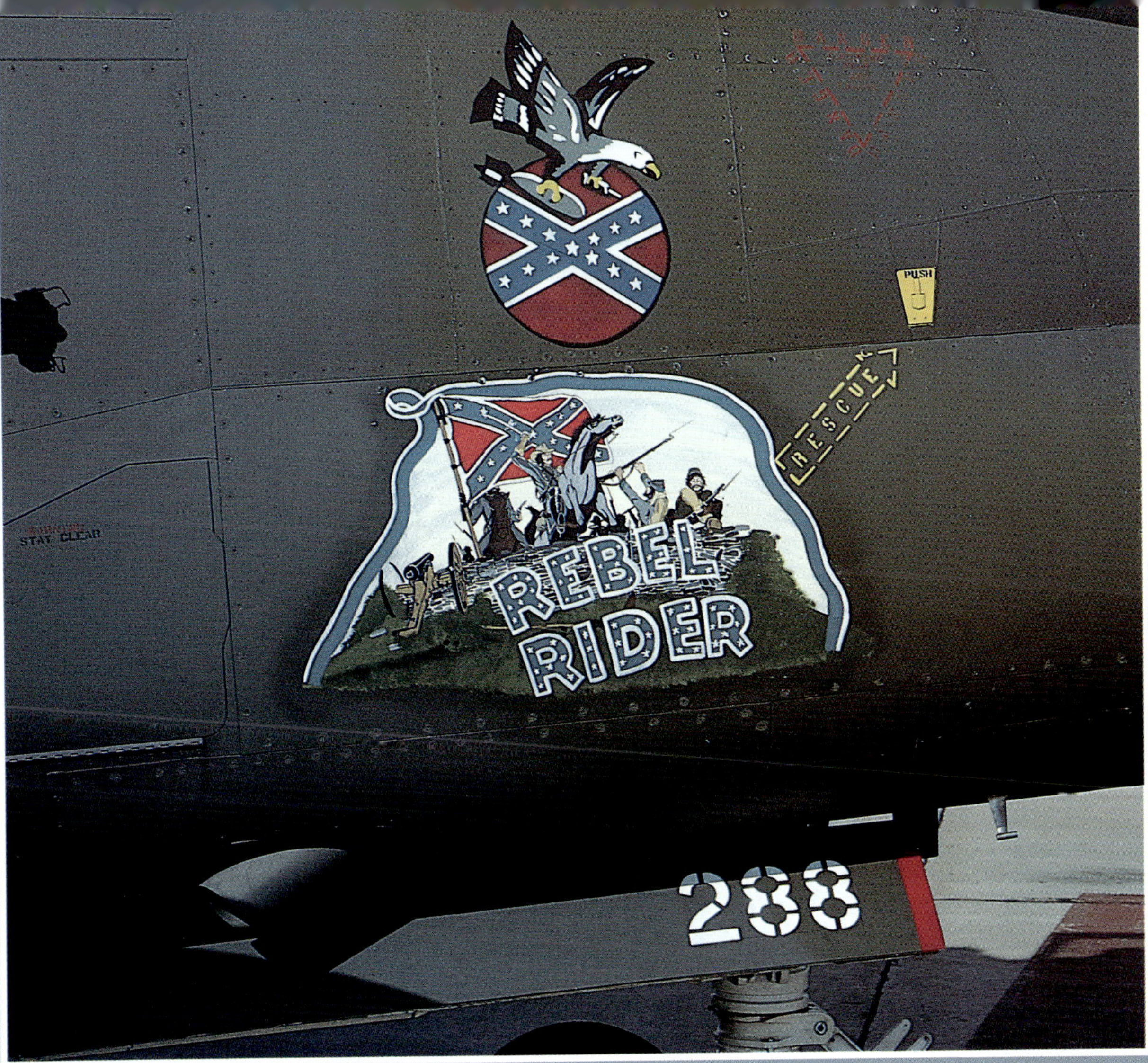
PUSH
RESCUE
REBEL RIDER
288

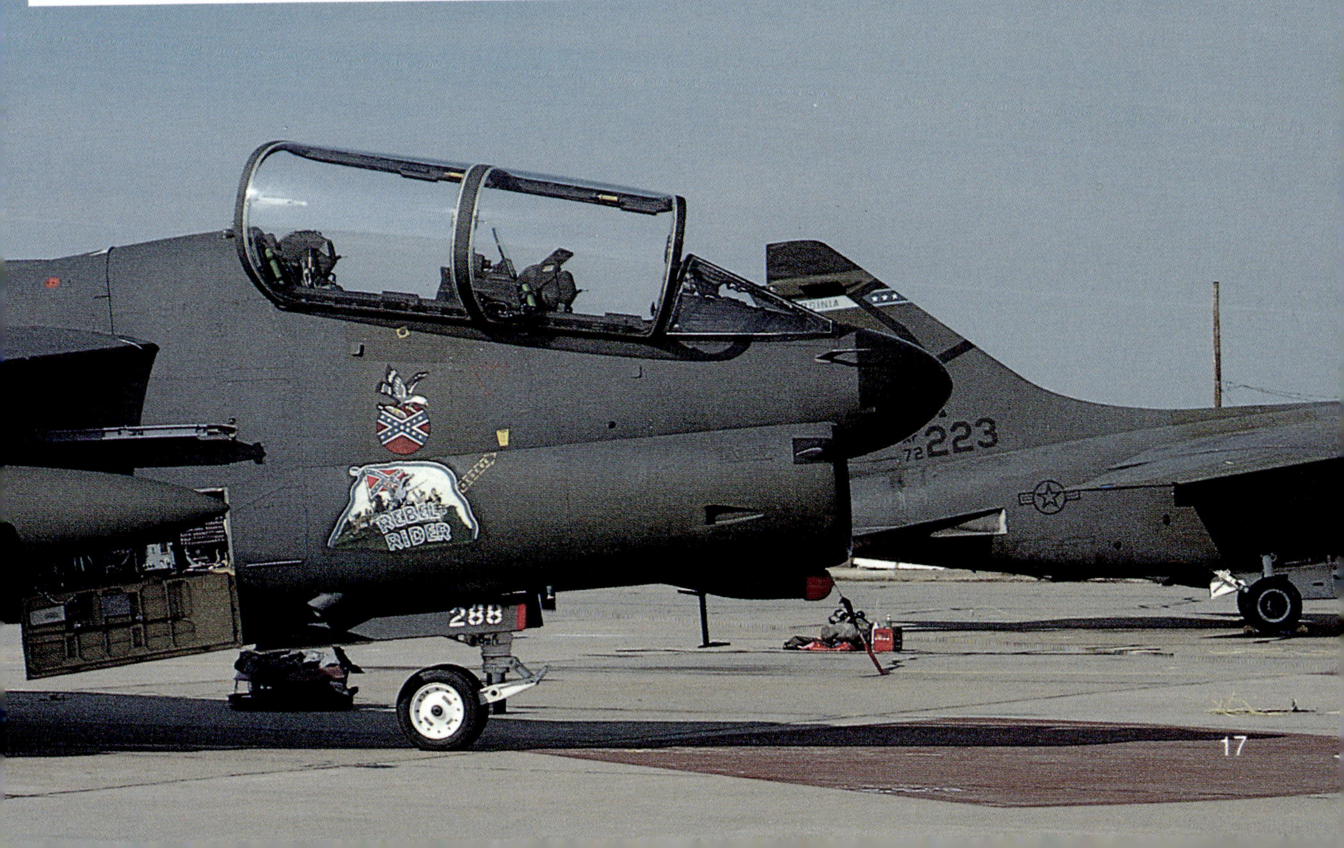
REBEL RIDER
288
223

Vought A-7K Corsair II (79-0461) of the 188th TFS, New Mexico ANG seen at Shaw AFB, South Carolina in February 1990, in the grey livery selected for this venerable airplane's final years of service.
(Norman Taylor)

Bullet Express appears in acrylic, rather than the nowadays more commonly used grease pencil, on the Fairchild A-10A Thunderbolt II (78-0592) which also bears the name of Colonel Sandy Sharpe, one of the US Air Force's most experienced air-to-ground tacticians. Sharpe commanded the 354th Tactical Fighter Wing (Provisional) at King Fahd Airport, Saudi Arabia during Operation "Desert Storm". His "Warthog" is seen here at Myrtle Beach AFB, South Carolina in May 1991 after returning from the war. Soon afterwards Myrtle Beach made the Pentagon's hit list for base closures; the 354th was scheduled to be disbanded, with its aircraft being parcelled out to other units. *(Norman Taylor)*

Play Time, an A-10A (78-0681) of the 353rd TFS, 354th TFW at Myrtle Beach AFB - note tail code - in late March 1991, shortly after returning from the Gulf. The nose art is very reminiscent of the classic 1940s approach. *(Norman Taylor)*

This Warthog (77-0268) belonged to the Air Force Reserve's 706th Tactical Fighter Squadron based at Naval Air Station New Orleans, Louisiana; it was photographed passing through Myrtle Beach AFB in May 1991. *Crescent City's Desert Darlyn* racked up quite a record in the Middle East: the A-10 was credited with five Iraqi tanks, three armored personnel carriers, five "triple-A" sites, two radar units, and six trucks. Note the Pave Penny laser guidance pod mounted on the off-center right side pylon beneath the cockpit. *(Norman Taylor)*

Nose art often projects little more than straightforward patriotism - even when it's slapped on the inside of the port side cockpit ladder door. This Warthog, (77-0238) of the 511th Fighter Squadron based at RAF Alconbury, England, is adorned with a simple testimony to Anglo-American comradeship - plus a rather poignant autograph. When he signed 77-0238 on 1 May 1990 Gen.Michael J.Dugan was Commander-in-Chief of US Air Forces in Europe (CINCUSAFE). An attack pilot himself, Dugan once said "I enjoy flying the A-10, because I'm a much more handsome aviator standing in front of an A-10 than I am standing in front of an F-16 or a B-1". When he became Chief of Staff on 1 July 1990, in an era of budgetary turmoil, the *Air Force Times* judged him "the man who can pilot the Air Force through the storm" - as it turned out, a sadly ironic choice of phrase by the time this photo was taken on 9 March 1992. On 18 September 1990, after eleven weeks in the job, Dugan was sacked for making public comments on USAF war plans during Operation "Desert Shield". Many feel that Dugan could have bolstered Air Force esprit de corps; some have alleged that a small injection of his sense of humor would not hurt his successor. The 511th FS has since deactivated. *(Norman Taylor)*

An historically authentic motif recalling one of the odder British Army fire support systems of the Victorian Imperial age is blazoned on this A-10A, *Have Gun, Will Travel* (79-0224) of the 509th Fighter Squadron, 10th Fighter Wing out of RAF Alconbury, England. It was photographed at Myrtle Beach AFB in January 1992. *(Norman Taylor)*

Warthog ladder door art of classic World War II style: A-10A (76-0527) of the 511th FS, 10th FW in March 1992. *(Norman Taylor)*

Ladder door interior of A-10A (79-188) of the 73rd Tactical Fighter Squadron, 23rd Tactical Fighter Wing at England AFB, Louisiana - since redesignated simply 23rd Wing, and transferred to Pope AFB, North Carolina. *(Kevin Foy)*

(Right) The ladder door of A-10A (79-0202) of the 23rd Wing shows how convoluted aircraft artwork can get. The tiger emblem at the top refers to the wing's historical link to the "Flying Tigers" - though the Chinese characters are bogus. Hans, Dave and Alex are crew chiefs and armorers of this A-10. Iraqi targets credited to the Hog's pilot in the Gulf, named Miller, are listed at right. "Storrman" refers to Captain Richard D.Storr, whose A-10 was shot down by Iraqi AAA on 2 February 1991. By the time 77-0202 was photographed at Myrtle Beach in November that year Storrman had long since returned from Iraqi captivity. *(Kevin Foy)*

HANS
DAVE
ALEX

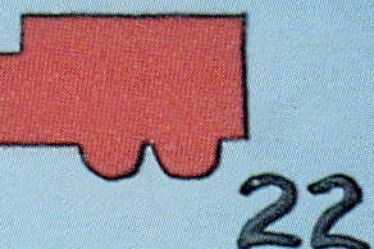
15

22
25

13

2

6
MILLER
FOR STORRMAN
WE'LL NEVER LET UP!

NG
DANGER
EJECTION SEAT
LIFT
DESERT STORM '91
JOINT FORCES
REMOVE BEFORE FLIGHT
BEFORE FLIGHT

(Left & below) This Hog (77-0205) of the 706th Tactical Fighter Squadron, an Air Force Reserve unit based at New Orleans, wears a complete set of the flags of the 27 nations of the Allied coalition in "Desert Storm" on its nosewheel door. The top item in its impressive kill tally is unusual: this is the aircraft in which Captain Robert R.Swain - a 33-year-old activated Reservist from Charlotte, NC, who normally flies Boeing 767s for USAir - shot down an Iraqi Boelkow Bo-105 helicopter with cannon fire on 6 February 1991. *(Norman Taylor)*

(Above) Saddam fleeing from Uncle's ordnance provides a fairly conventional subject for the artwork on A-10A (77-0271) *Holy ***t!* of the 706th Tactical Fighter Squadron; but the origins of the bellicose prawn on its squadron-mate *Desert Storm* (77-0269) are more obscure. Both were photographed at Myrtle Beach AFB in May 1991. *(Norman Taylor)*

(Above & Right) This A-10A (79-0163) of the 354th TFW's 355th TFS - note insignia behind cockpit - proved to be a terrible swift sword indeed for Saddam Hussein's luckless legions. The white "I" on the nose of this unit's Hogs is a guide for the boom operators of tanker aircraft. *(Norman Taylor)*

OA-10A (76-0529) *Mary Jane* of the 23rd Tactical Air Support Squadron, photographed at Davis-Monthan AFB, Arizona, on 19 May 1991, displays impeccably patriotic and tasteful nose art incorporating the flag, the Statue of Liberty, and a map of the continental USA - shame about Alaska and Hawaii. Some USAF A-10s have since appeared in gray camouflage, although lizard green remains standard for most. *(Norman Taylor)*

MB

PLT CAPT JACK W THOMAS
DCC SSGT DUSTY M MILLAR
ACC SGT GEORGE L LOFTEN
163

Four more Warthog muzzles from the 23rd TASS: (76-0537) *Angel/Bad to the Bone;* (76-0547) *The Unknown Bomber;* (77-0183) *Wild Thing;* and (77-0185) *Lenni May.* Davis-Monthan AFB, May 1991. *(Norman Taylor)*

183
Wild Thing
WARNING
ENGINE RUN UP, TAXI, OR FLIGHT IS PROHIBITED WITH BATTERY CIRCUIT BREAKERS PULLED IF FAULT HAS CAUSE TRIP, REPAIR CAUSE AND IMMEDIATLY RESET

Live to Fly
185
Fly to Kill
Lenni May
WARNING
ENGINE RUN UP, TAXI, OR FLIGHT IS PROHIBITED WITH BATTERY CIRCUIT BREAKERS PULLED IF FAULT HAS CAUSE TRIP, REPAIR CAUSE AND IMMEDIATLY RESET

Raven
SF
229

Memphis Belle
III

A-10A (80-0229) of the 21st Fighter Squadron, 507th Air Control Wing, pictured at Shaw AFB, South Carolina in November 1991. This Hog is thought to share its main artwork, honoring the immortal Flying Fortress of the old 91st Bomb Group, with a B-52 of today's 2nd Wing - though not, one assumes, the secondary emblem lurking inside the ladder door. ***(Norman Taylor)***

RESCUE
DANGER
EJECTION SEAT
DANGER
DANGER
WARNING
THIS AIRPLANE CONTAINS SEAT EJECTION AND CANOPY JETTISON INITIATORS CONTAINING EXPLOSIVE CHARGES
2
RESCUE
STEAL YOUR FACE

Raven
SF
507 ACW
964

Steal Your Face is the sinister promise made by OA-10A (81-0964), in November 1991 the 507th Air Control Wing commander's ship, its fins enlivened with the "Raven" flash above the Shaw Field tail code. This outfit were originally forward air controllers flying clandestine missions over Laos in the 1960s. *(Norman Taylor)*

A December 1991 selection of OA-10A blazons from the 507th ACW's 21st Fighter Squadron: *Desert Belle* (81-0947), *Hog's Breath Saloon* (80-0657), *Annabelle II* (80-0208), and *Desert Dream* (80-0277) - the latter a homage to Marilyn Monroe's most famous pose. ***(Norman Taylor)***

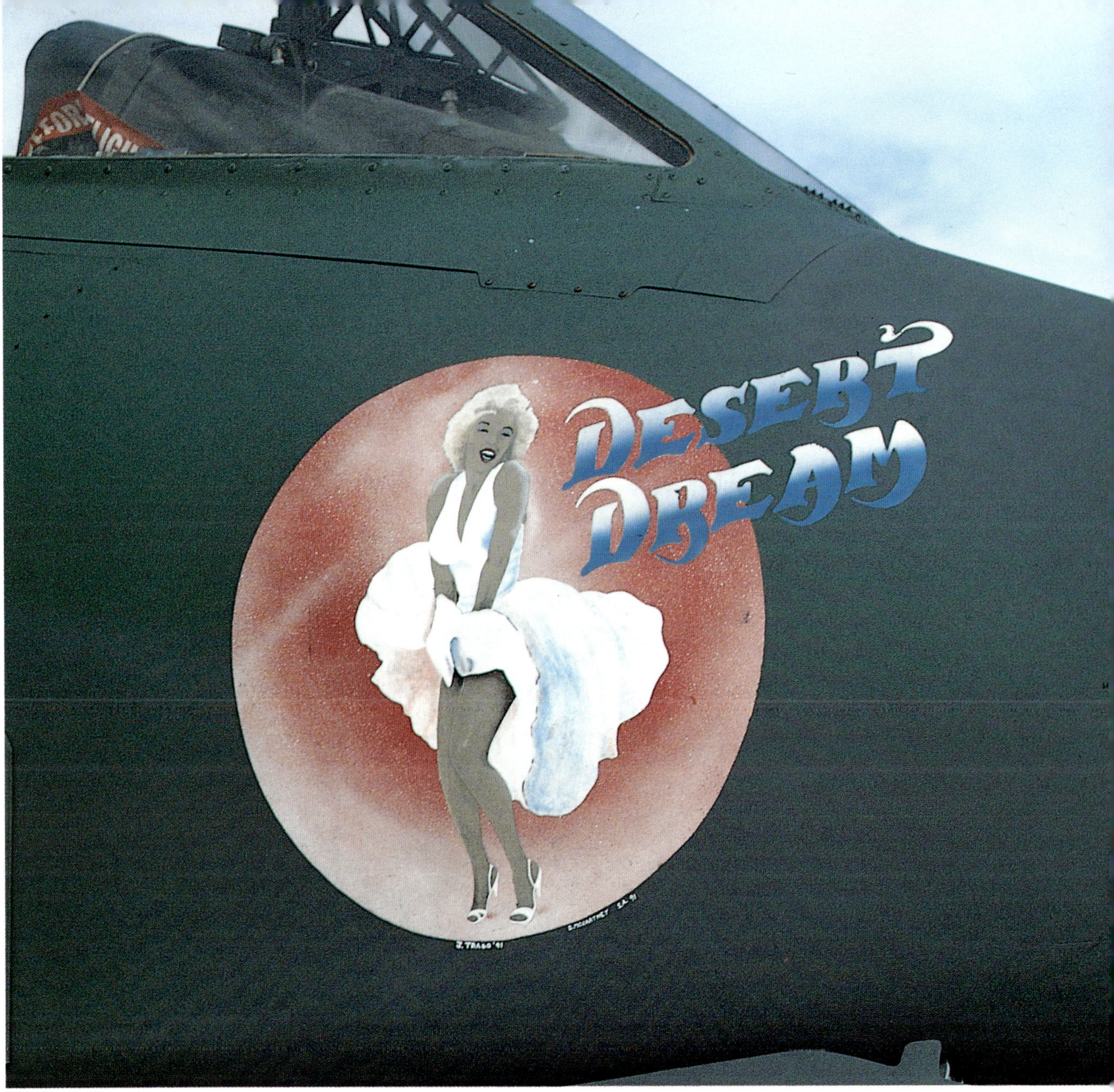
DESERT DREAM

DANGER
EJECTION SEAT
DANGER
WARNING
ANNABELLE II

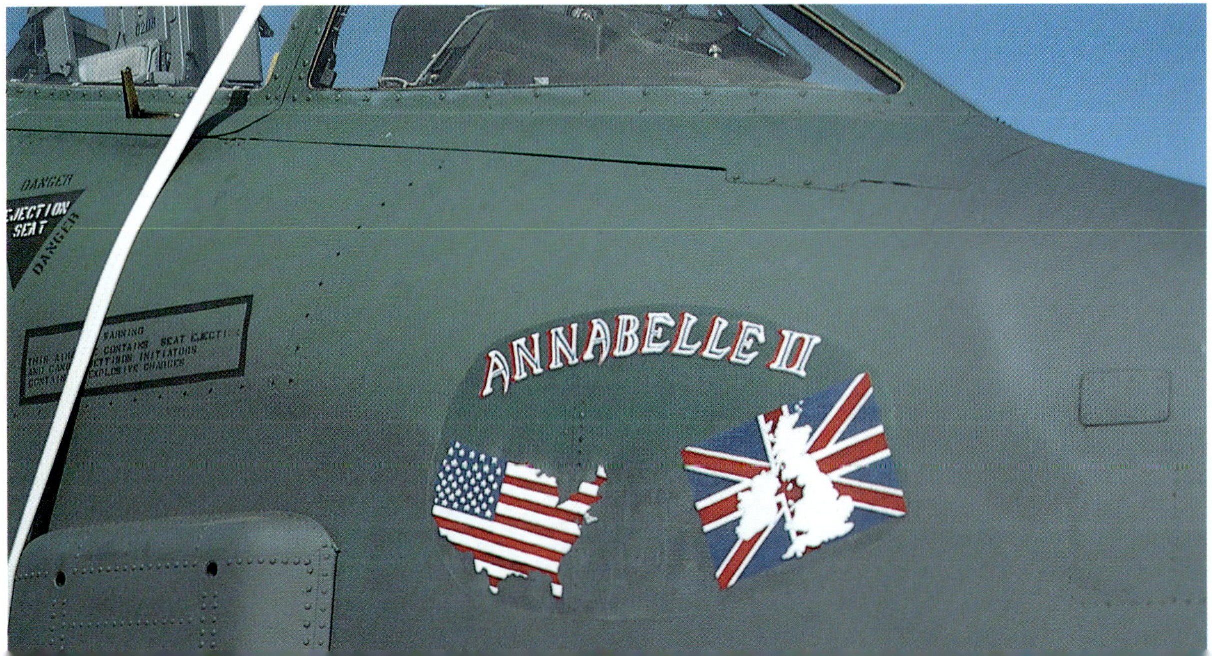

Stratotankers in Splendour

The "data block" on the left of the forward fuselage of USAF aircraft is frequently inaccurate: this one should say KC-135E, not KC-135/E. This camouflaged Boeing Stratotanker (56-6341) from the 117th Air Refueling Squadron, Kansas ANG, has borrowed the character Wiley E.Coyote from the famous "Roadrunner" cartoons, transforming the world's best-known user of Acme products into a flying gas station. One doubts if even this lighthearted nose art, photographed in October 1990, will survive a 23 July 1992 Air Mobility Command decree: "All AMC nose art will reflect a theme of civic/community pride, be distinctive, symbolic, and designed and maintained to the highest quality standards. Designs will be gender-neutral..." *(Jerry Geer)*

ACME JET
HI TEST
kī-ō'tē-əs găs'-ē-əs
SERIAL NO.56-3641
3641
STATIC PORTS

Swift Hawk is a KC-135R Stratotanker (63-7979) of the llth ARS, 340th ARW photographed in March 1990 at Altus AFB, Oklahoma; aptly for the state which was once Indian Territory, she bears a shield-and-pipe motif. Stratotankers which are not dark-camouflaged wear this attractive pearl-gray aluminized paint scheme. Altus is expected to become the training base for the KC-135 in the mid- to late 1990s. *(Jerry Geer)*

(Right, above) Several variations on the insanely voracious cartoon character Tazz, the Tasmanian Devil, have brightened tankers like this Boeing KC-135E (57-1460) seen at Forbes Field, Kansas, in October 1991 after "Desert Storm". Camouflaged tankers are perhaps less pleasing to the eye than those left in natural metal/gray (and much hotter inside on a sunny day); but this veteran of the 117th ARS, Kansas ANG, offers some entertainment. The red Pegasus, formerly the logo of the Mobil Oil Company, has been transformed into a camel and has acquired a refueling boom; its Persian Gulf operations tally features black camels for peacetime, red for wartime "flying gas station" missions. The crew chiefs get billing - important for morale - on a blue block above the mission tally. *(Jerry Geer)*

(Right) At Kunsan AB, Korea, where the potential for conflict has not yet faded with the Cold War, KC-135Q Stratotanker (58-0050) wears a *Spook* reminding us of Hollywood's Caspar the Friendly Ghost, who seems to be trapped inside the serial number. The KC-135Q model was intended to carry special fuel for the now-retired SR-71 Blackbird, but has long since reverted to the same standard as the "plain vanilla" KC-135A. This ship was visiting Korea in November 1991 from the 380th ARS at Plattsburgh AFB, New York. (*Paul Hunt)*

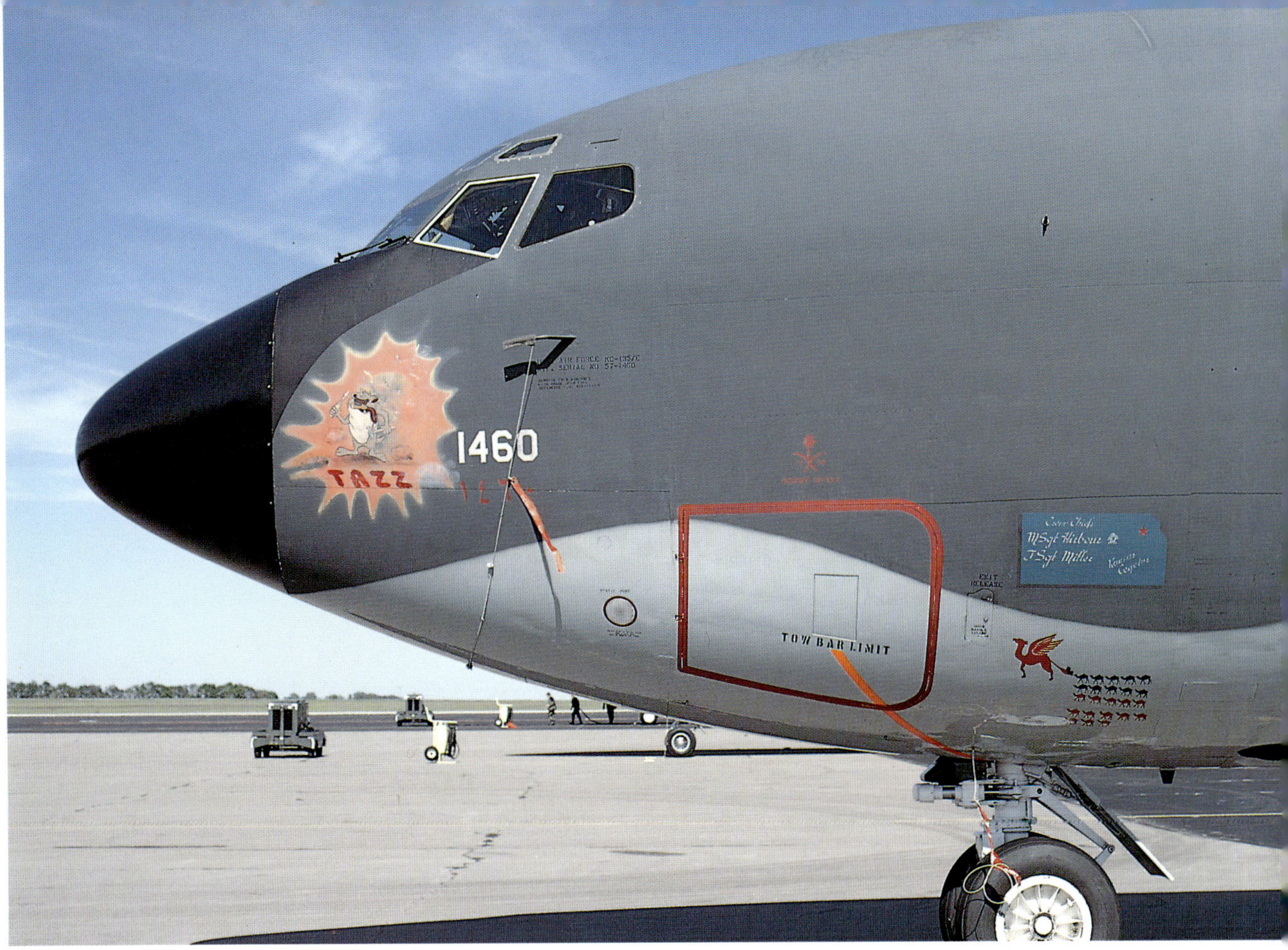
TAZZ
1460
TOW BAR LIMIT

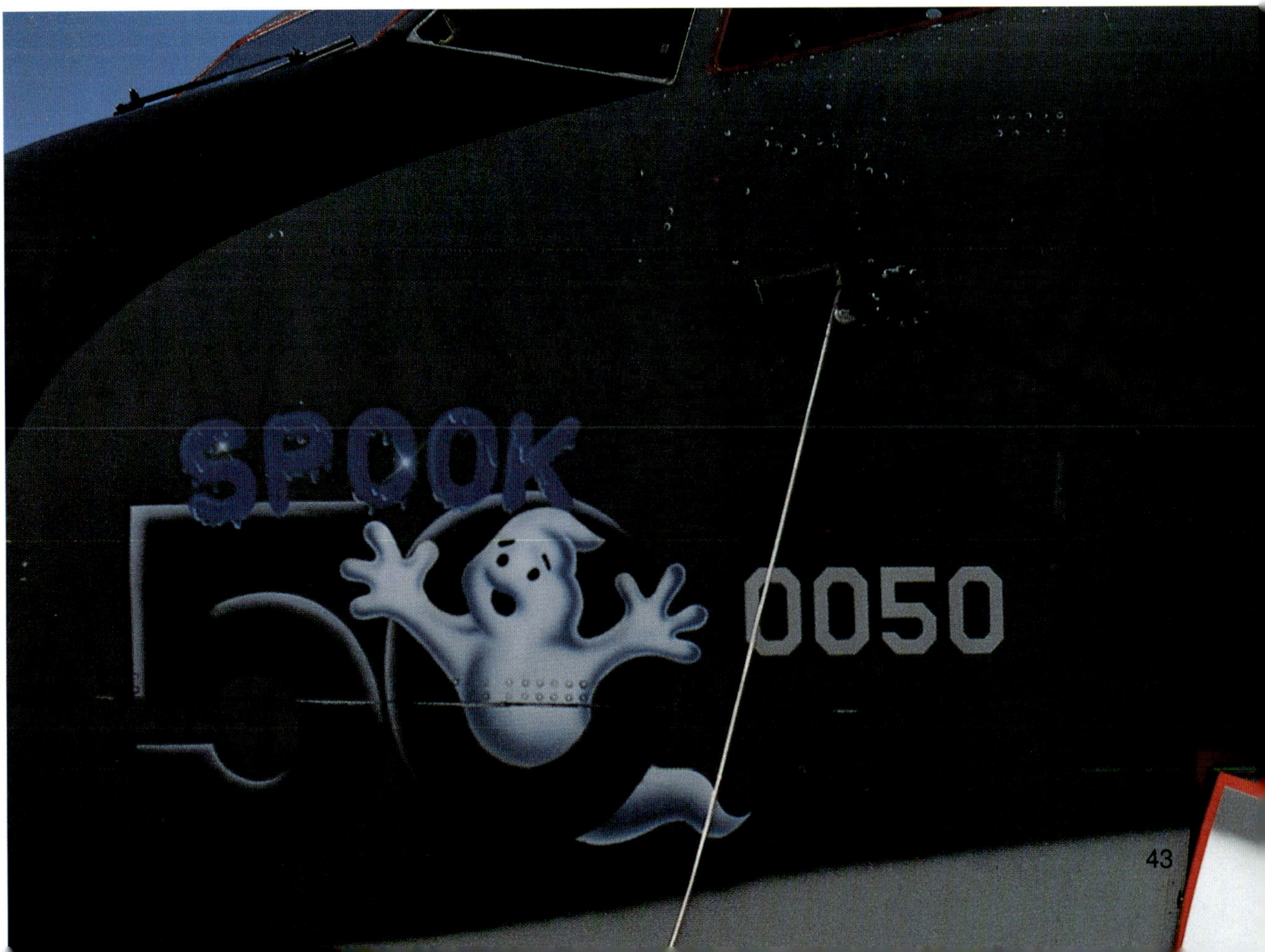
SPOOK
0050

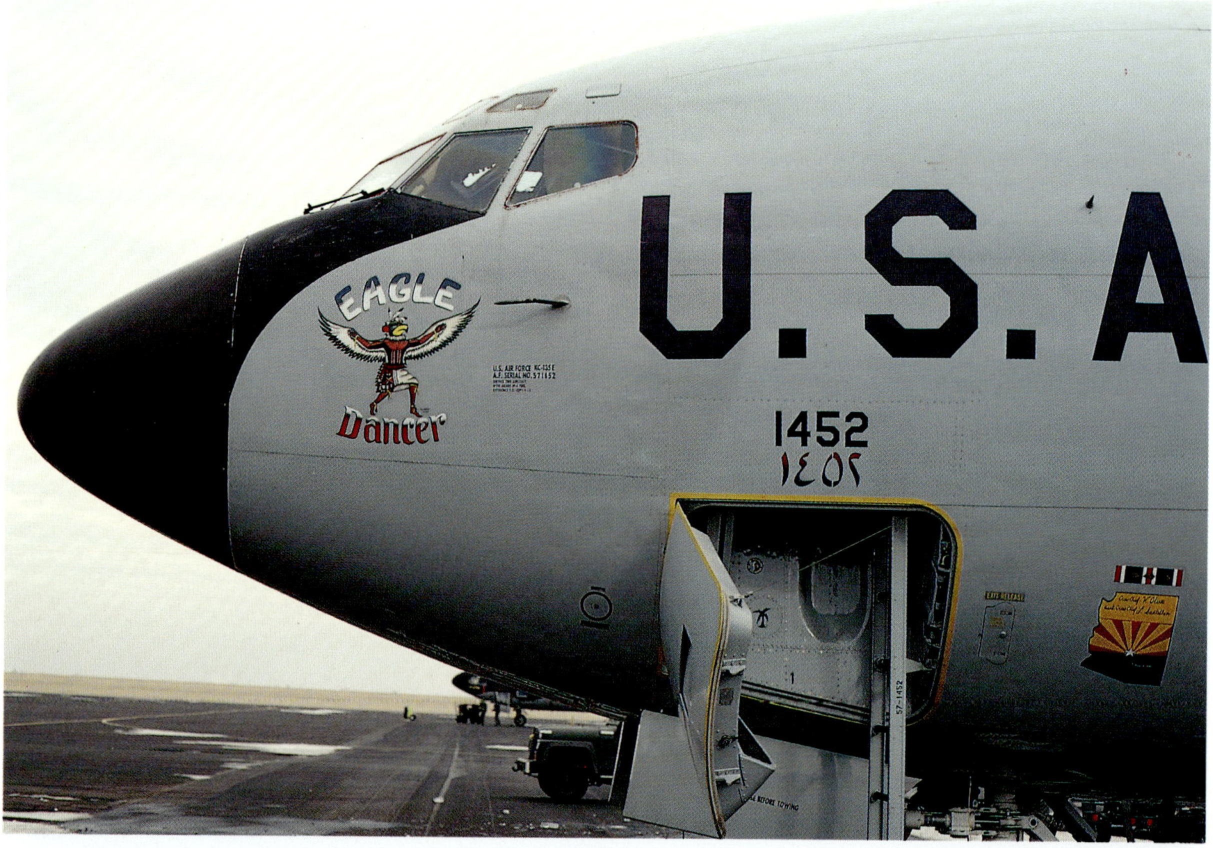
EAGLE
Dancer
1452
U.S.A

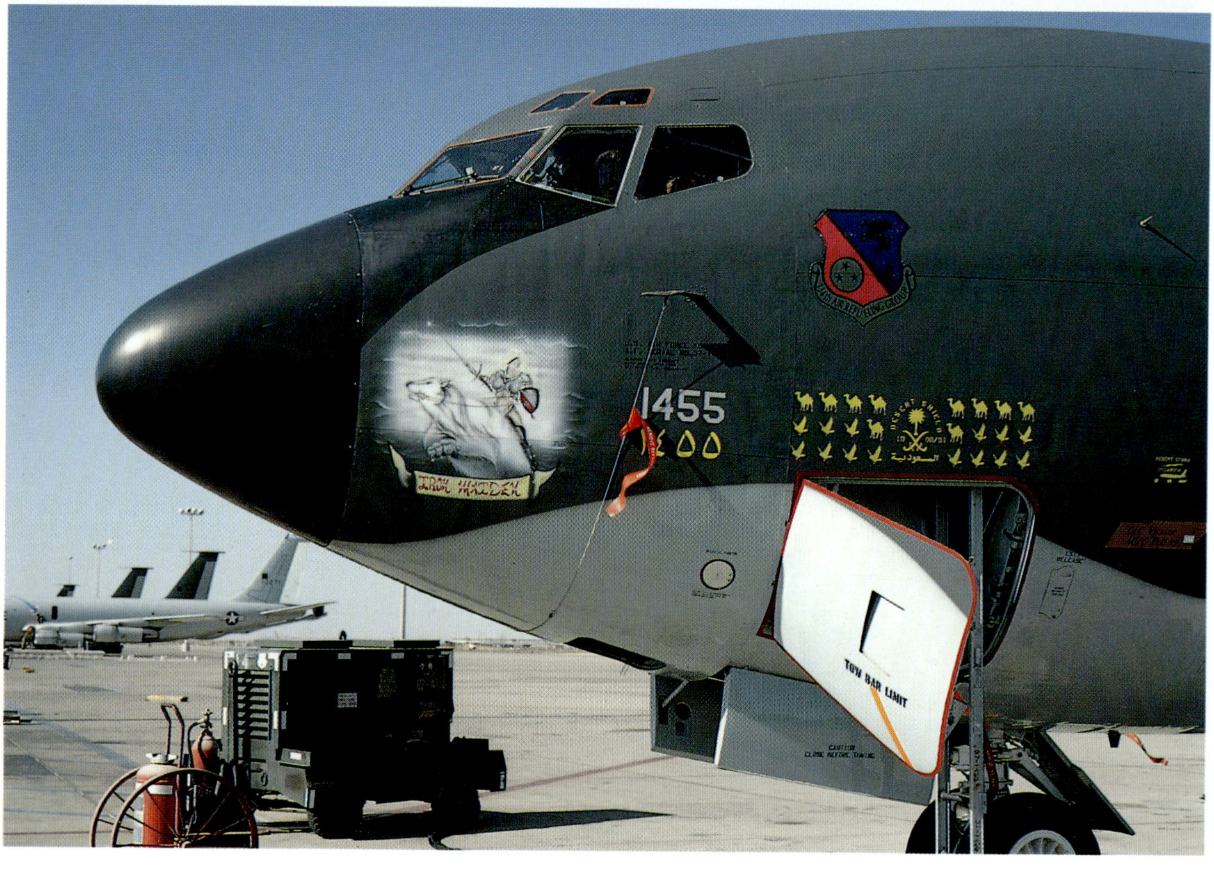
IRON MAIDEN
1455
TOW BAR LIMIT

(Left, above) Another, and particularly nicely rendered Native American motif adorns *Eagle Dancer,* a KC-135E (57-1452) belonging to the 197th ARS, Arizona ANG, stationed at Phoenix Sky Harbor. The star/sunburst below the unit citation bar behind the entry door is a version of the Arizona flag within an outline of the Grand Canyon State. Seen on a visit to Forbes Field, Kansas, in December 1990, this Stratotanker is obviously a "Desert Shield" veteran - note the Arabic digit repetition of the "last four" above the door. *(Jerry Geer)*

(Left, below) *Iron Maiden* carries a variety of artwork, including a proud tally of "Desert Shield/Storm" hash marks and an Arabic translation of the "last four" in a yellow shade set off nicely by the dark camouflage. This KC-135E (57-1455) belongs to the Knoxville-based 134th Air Refueling Group, Tennessee ANG; the unit decal passes the test of the postwar Taste Police - the Maiden herself sadly flunks it. *(Brian C.Rogers)*

...And so, probably, does *Work'n Girl,* a KC-135E (58-0006) of the 191st ARG, Utah ANG seen at Gulfport, Mississippi in March 1992. Gender-neutral she ain't; but Lord knows how many people who have any business on an air base would actually be offended by this 1950s waitress from one of the drive-ins which abounded in the days when Elvis was King, but which are as hard to find today as a decent meal or decent service. *(Brian C.Rogers)*

The Spirit of Kitty Hawk, **with its artwork honoring the Wright brothers' first flight, is a Douglas KC-10A Extender dual role tanker/transport; (87-0124) of the 344th ARS, 4th Wing, based at Seymour Johnson AFB, South Carolina, was photographed in May 1991.** ***(Norman Taylor)***

The 911th Air Refueling Squadron, another unit of the 4th Wing at Seymour Johnson, operates KC-10A *Shady "J" Express* (86-0038). *(Norman Taylor)*

Falcons Forever

Hawg Heaven, posed here with its crew chief, is a two-seat General Dynamics F-16B block 10 Fighting Falcon (78-0104) assigned to the 184th Fighter Group, Kansas ANG at McConnell AFB, Kansas. The name was applied to this "Electric Jet" (as the F-16 is sometimes known because of its fly-by-wire controls) at about the time that an F-16 in another unit had a bizarre and widely-enjoyed accident: the pilot was forced to eject after a collision on the ground with a pig! Typical of contemporary markings, although in low-visibility gray, are the Air National Guard emblem and state name on the tail. *(Jerry Geer)*

The military keeps its aircraft colorless, partly because bureaucracy doesn't understand esprit de corps but mostly because even the smallest splash of color can be a red flag for an infrared missile. Still, even when they are limited to only two colors - gray and gray - some airmen find ways to broadcast a mission. This F-16C Fighting Falcon (86-0242) belongs to the 149th Fighter Squadron, Virginia ANG - the same outfit which has now eschewed the Confederate battle flag. While serving with another unit 0242 flew 34 combat sorties in Operation "Desert Storm", seen recorded by falcon silhouettes behind the cockpit during a visit to McEntire ANG Base, South Carolina on 30 October 1991. *(Norman Taylor)*

(Above & right) For the next few pages the reader enters the nose art equivalent of the Louvre: pay attention - we are in the presence of genius, and his name is Staff Sergeant Warren Trask II. *Sweet... but Deadly!* is a General Dynamics F-16C (83-1158) of the 363rd Tactical Fighter Wing's 33rd TFS, the "Falcons" (note tail band). Of the two squadrons sent to war by this wing, the 33rd ranged the Gulf skies blazoned with tasteful, vivid, and often unmistakably female motifs grease-pencilled by Trask, while some ships of the 17th TFS wore more macabre images from a darker creative talent. This F-16C was photographed at Shaw AFB, South Carolina, on 24 April 1991, weeks after it returned from "Desert Storm" and days before the wartime artwork was ordered removed. The words "philistine" and "vandal" spring to mind....*(Robert F.Dorr)*

More conventional World War II-style "hash marks" record the 35 missions flown by Captain John "Barney" Fyfe's F-16C block 30 Fighting Falcon (84-0262) with the 363rd Tactical Fighter Wing in the Middle East. *(Kevin Foy)*

FALCONS
SW
AF 83 158
RESCUE
FALCONS
SW
AF 83 146

DANGER
EJECTION SEAT
DANGER
DANGER

Staff Sergeant Trask decorated an entire squadron's F-16s for the war in the desert, even though he had never taken a single class in art. An officer told Trask what to do with a regulation which called for the submission of proposed nose art to a higher headquarters for approval: "Ignore it". Much of Trask's work consisted of female figures sketched in lusty but cheerful good taste; but this non-com Michelangelo's shining moment came when he decorated his wing commander's F-16C (85-1419) - veteran of 57 missions in the Gulf. It is hard to believe that this intricate, detailed symbol of unit pride and patriotism was accomplished entirely with grease pencil - but here are the photos to prove it. ***(David F.Brown/Norman Taylor/Robert F.Dorr)***

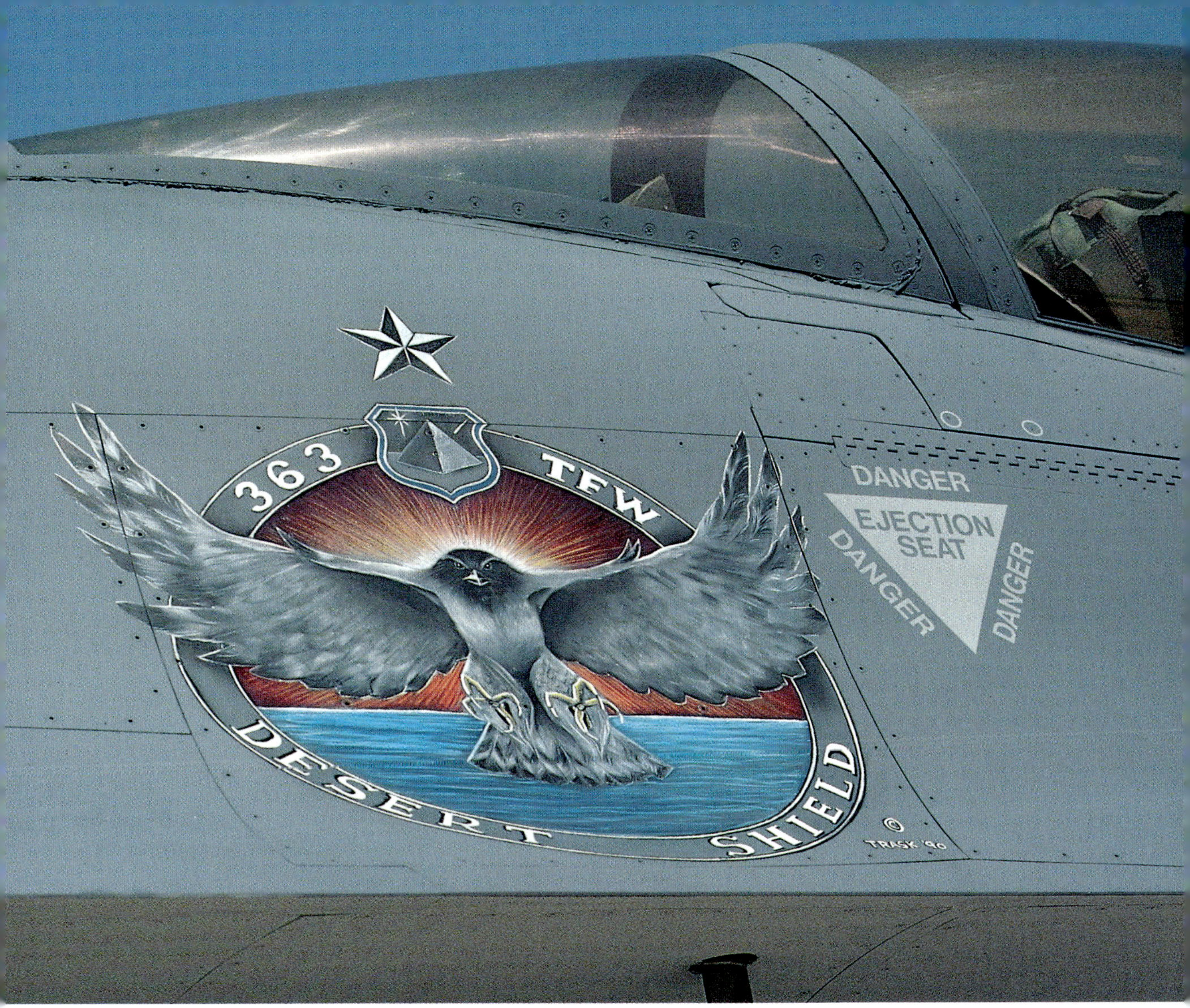

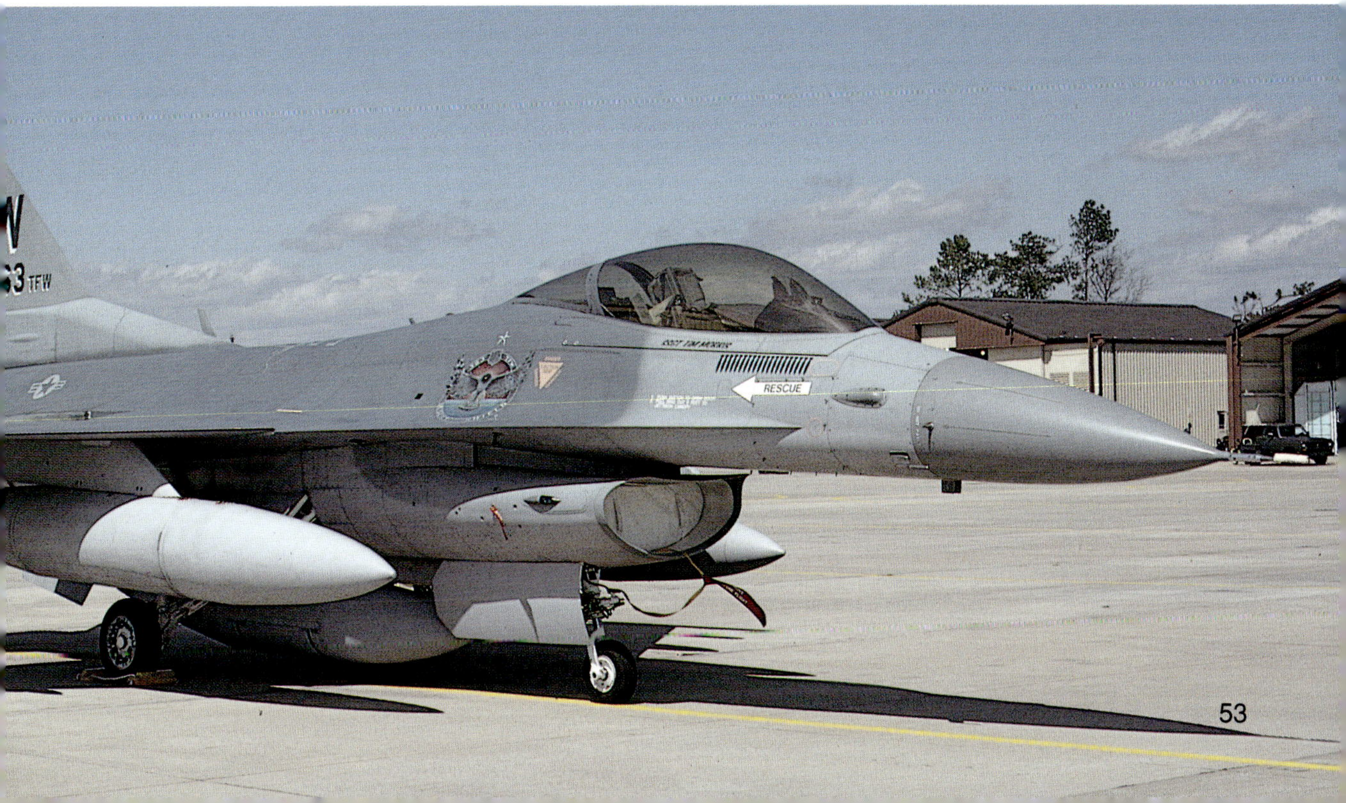

(Above & left) *Wild Child,* a nickname which reflects both a popular rock song and an approach to flying, is F-16C (84-1265) of the 33rd TFS, 363rd TFW; this raygun-happy character flew 43 combat missions during "Desert Storm". Note also the subdued warning triangle for the ejection seat. *(Norman Taylor)*

(Right, above & below) F-16C (83-1150) *Max Thrust* flew 50 missions in the Gulf with the 33rd TFS, even though only 14 black bomb symbols are visible in this March 1991 photograph. Apart from the Trask artwork, note the 363rd TFW decal on the intake. *(Norman Taylor)*

Trask decorated F-16C (83-1142) *Harmful F/X* - "effects" - with a survivalist theme. It must have worked: 1142 came home safe to Shaw AFB after flying 42 combat missions in "Desert Storm". *(Norman Taylor)*

(Below & right) F-16C (85-1420) *Code One Candy,* a 33rd TFS ship with the classic Trask touch. A "code one" is an aircraft reported by its pilot to have no mechanical problems. *(Norman Taylor)*

"CODE-ONE" CANDY
DANGER
EJECTION
SEAT
DANGER
DANGER

(Above & below) The 17th TFS "Hooters" also performed well with the 363rd TFW in "Desert Storm". F-16C (84-1223), photographed at Shaw AFB in March 1991, is a "boss bird" for the 17th's Aviation Maintenance Unit (note tail marking), and bears a suitable emblem. *(Norman Taylor)*

(Above & below) F-16C (84-1254) of the 17th TFS bears artwork typical of the slightly more macabre trend favored by this squadron: a medieval headsman calling *"Next..."* This Falcon flew 38 combat missions in the Gulf. *(Norman Taylor)*

(Above & right) The Michael Keeton movie "Batman" was popular at about the time when this F-16C (83-1159) of the 17th TFS racked up 45 missions in "Desert Storm", wearing the caped crusader's menacing logo. *(Norman Taylor)*

(Above & right) *War Wench,* F-16C (84-1247), is a 37-mission Gulf veteran of the 17th TFS, 363rd TFW. *(Norman Taylor)*

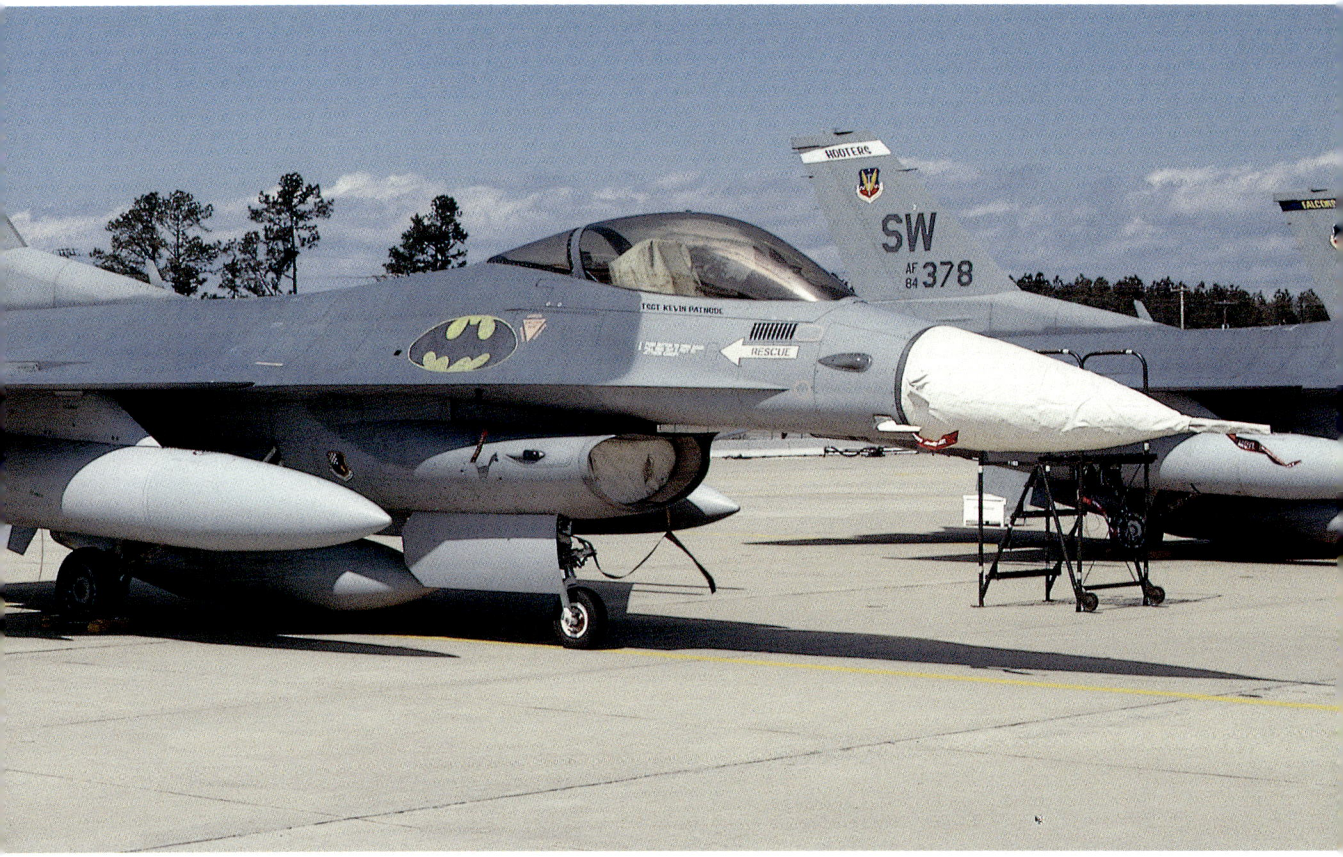
HOOTERS
SW
AF
84 378
RESCUE

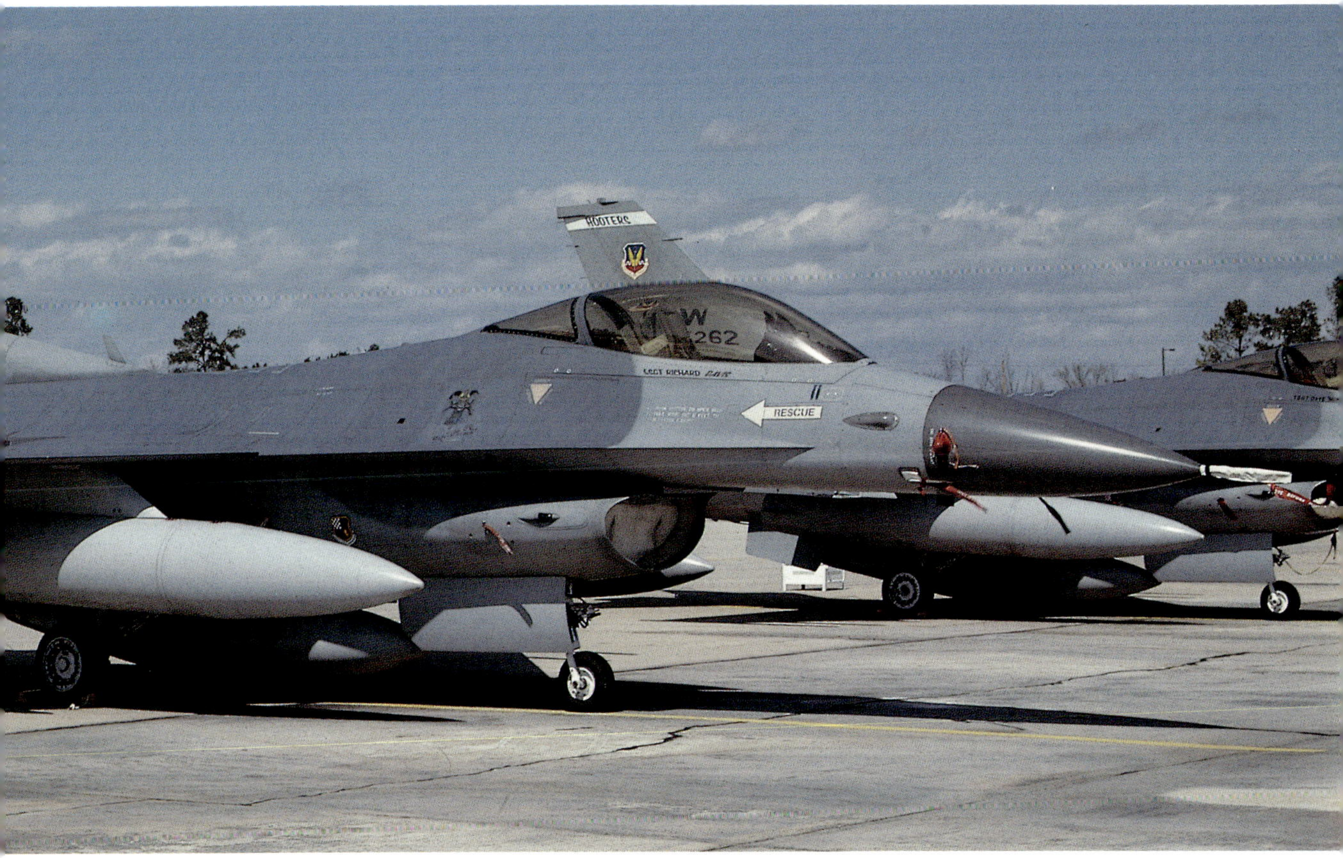
HOOTERS
RESCUE

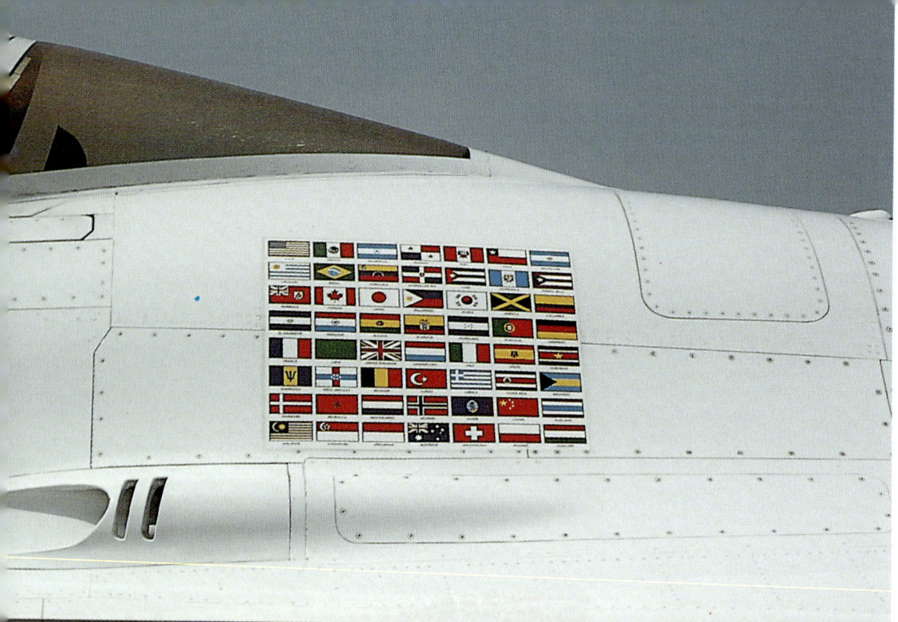

The F-16 Fighting Falcon has entertained supporters of the United States Air Force in something like 60 countries (note the flags on aircraft no.5) in the hands of the USAF Thunderbirds flight display team. The Thunderbirds are based at Nellis AFB, Nevada; they were photographed here at Myrtle Beach AFB, South Carolina, in June 1992. At the beginning of the 1992 season they traded in their F-15A/B block 15 aircraft, modified with P&W F100-PW-2320 engines, for F-16C/D block 45 models. On the Thunderbirds' aircraft the space normally occupied by the cannon is filled instead by an oil tank used to make smoke for airshow displays. Aircraft no.5 wears its individual number upside down because, during the solo performances which break up four-plane routines, it makes fast inverted passes. *(Norman Taylor)*

AMC
50269
U.S. AIR FORCE

Artistic Airlifters

Beginning in early 1992 Air Mobility Command (AMC) began the gradual replacement of the lizard green or "Europe One" camouflage on its airlifters with the "AMC proud gray" paint scheme shown here; a semi-gloss paint was adopted after a gloss type was tested and found difficult to maintain. By late the same year AMC had also adopted the practice - previously limited to KC-135 tankers - of applying colored tail bands to its transports. This Lockheed C-141B Starlifter (65-0269) of the 437th Airlift Wing out of Charleston AFB, South Carolina, seen here at Mombasa, Kenya in November 1992, incorporates both these changes. *(Robert F.Dorr)*

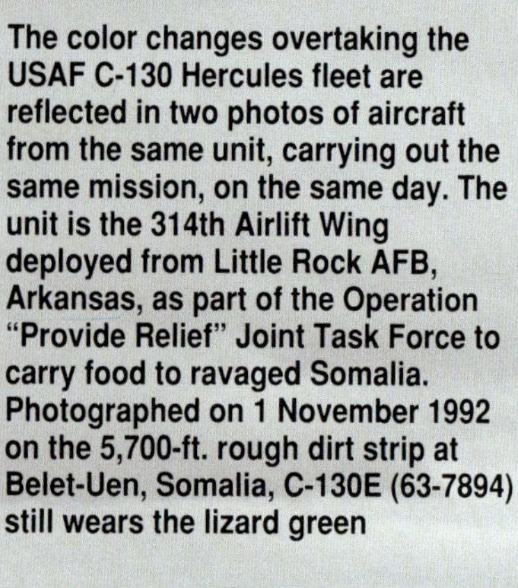

The color changes overtaking the USAF C-130 Hercules fleet are reflected in two photos of aircraft from the same unit, carrying out the same mission, on the same day. The unit is the 314th Airlift Wing deployed from Little Rock AFB, Arkansas, as part of the Operation "Provide Relief" Joint Task Force to carry food to ravaged Somalia. Photographed on 1 November 1992 on the 5,700-ft. rough dirt strip at Belet-Uen, Somalia, C-130E (63-7894) still wears the lizard green camouflage current since the early 1980s; C-130E (64-10948) wears the new "proud gray"; both have Red Cross emblems hastily applied to the fin bases with tape. The American flag on the fin is a new addition for most C-130s; it was decided to apply it to the whole fleet after a tragic mishap on 24 April 1992 when Peruvian fighters fired on a USAF C-130H (67-7183) flying a counter-drug mission, killing one crew member. *(Robert F.Dorr)*

1288
374 TAW

Lady Sheryl, Storm Rider, clearly a veteran of "Desert Storm", is a Lockheed C-130E Hercules (72-1288) of the 374th Tactical Airlift Wing seen at Kunsan AB, Korea, in September 1991. The wing, which has since lost the modifier "Tactical", is garrisoned at Yokota AB, Japan. A spokesman for Pacific Air Forces (PACAF) was unable to say whether his command has issued an edict restricting nose art to the patriotic and "tasteful"; but whether or not a specific order has been issued the witch-hunt against "gender specific" art is general throughout the Air Force, and it is unlikely that *Sheryl* survives today. *(Paul Hunt)*

With the redesignation of the 23rd Wing as a "composite" formation the A-10A Warthogs were joined by C-130 Hercules; and since the 23rd can legitimately trace its lineage to the AVG "Flying Tigers" of World War II, the Hercs too may now sport the historic shark's teeth. C-130E (63-9810) was photographed at the 23rd's home base, Pope AFB near Fayetteville, North Carolina, in June 1992. *(Norman Taylor)*

(Right) *Desert Phoenix*, a Lockheed C-130E Hercules (64-0502) of the 37th Tactical Airlift Squadron, 435th Tactical Airlift Wing from Rhein-Main air base at Frankfurt, Germany, was photographed during deployment to Saudi Arabia in February 1992. The impressively rendered nose art was applied - like much of that seen during "Desert Storm" - with grease pencil, and seems susceptible to wear and tear. *(Brandon Middleton)*

(Above & right) Late-model AC-130 Spectre gunships, converted Lockheed C-130 Hercules airframes fitted by Rockwell with a terrifying broadside of 105mm and multi-barrel 40mm and 20mm cannon, are as valued today as were their Vietnam War predecessors "Puff" and "Spooky". Ten AC-130H Spectre IIs from the 1st Special Operations Wing flew to the Gulf early in "Desert Shield", as did others from the Air Force Reserve. This AC-130U Spectre (87-0128), undergoing development work with the 6510th Test Wing at Edwards AFB, California, in October 1991, displays suitably ominous nose art. *(Craig Kaston)*

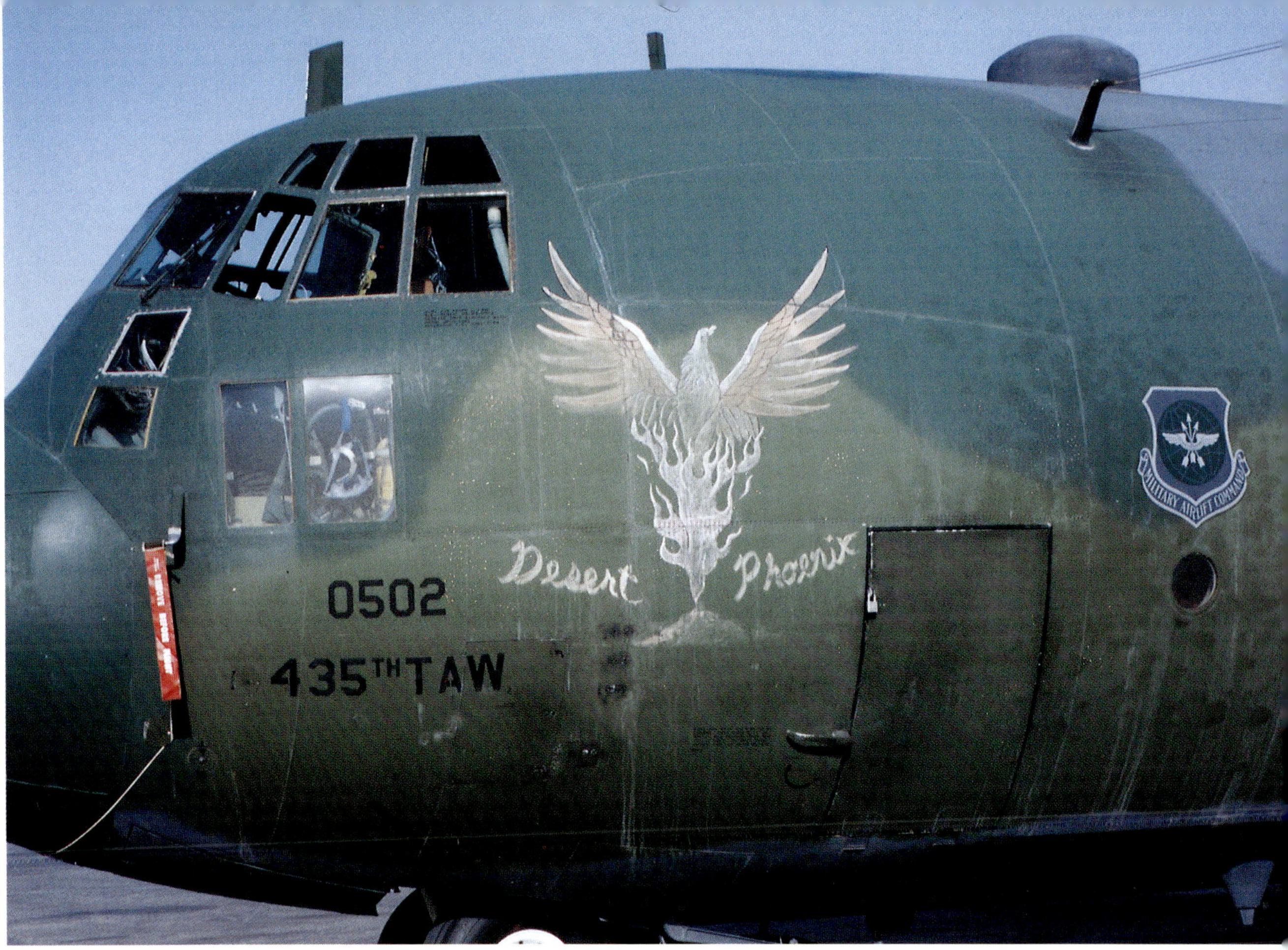
Desert Phoenix
0502
435TH TAW
MILITARY AIRLIFT COMMAND

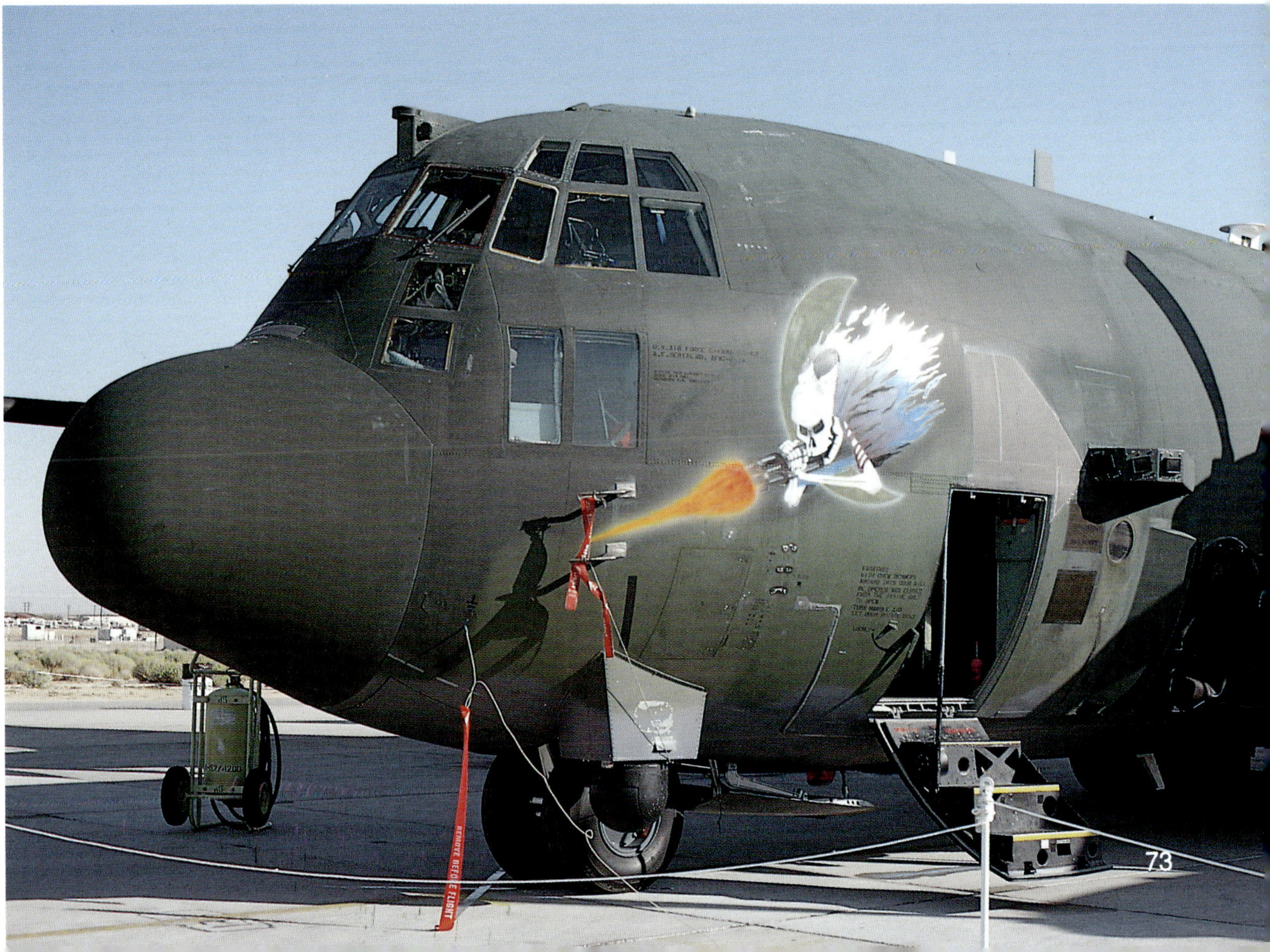

B is for Bomber

Boeing B-52G Stratofortress (60-0016) of the 7th Bomb Wing at Carswell AFB, Texas, in August 1990 bearing not only nose art but also a silhouette of the Lone Star State. In February 1991 co-author Robert F. Dorr flew a nine-hour low-level bombing mission in *Junkyard Dog* out of Carswell, a base which was identified for closure soon afterwards. *(Brian C.Rogers)*

American Eagle, here inflicting harm on an adversary of decidedly Red hues, is a B-52H Stratofortress (61-0015), one of the very last manufactured. It belongs to the 416th Bomb Wing - whose decal insignia has become somewhat frayed - and was photographed at Forbes AFB, Kansas, in October 1991. *(Jerry Geer)*

(Below) Flyers are traditionally superstitious; but there is solid World War II 8th AAF precedent for spitting in the devil's eye like this...

B-52 Stratofortress (58-0236) *Lucky 13* of the 2nd Bomb Wing - since renamed just 2nd Wing as a "composite" bomber and tanker formation of the new Air Combat Command - located at Barksdale AFB, Louisiana, in September 1991 bears a state map outline enclosing the names of the crew chiefs. *(Jerry Geer)*

Bridesmaid Becky, a B-52H (60-0043) of the 410th Bomb Wing at Whiteman AFB, Missouri, in August 1990. *(Jerry Geer)*

(Below) *The Witch II*, another 2nd Bomb Wing Stratofortress; during Operation "Desert Storm" this B-52G (58-0181) operated with the temporary 801st Bomb Wing out of Moron, Spain, and logged 23 combat missions against Iraq.

In the mid-1990s the USAF is contemplating transferring some of the older B-52 "Buffs" (Big Ugly Fat Fellows) to Air National Guard and Air Force Reserve units, both of which are integral to war-fighting plans and participate regularly in exercises and real-life operations. *(Brian C.Rogers)*

The Moose is Loose, a B-52G (58-0253) belonging to the 42nd Bomb Wing, seen at Tinker AFB, Oklahoma in May 1992 - the final month of Strategic Air Command's 47-year existence. The Moose's declared "Appetite for Destruction" - see crew chief name box - is confirmed by no less than 52 combat mission markers from "Desert Storm". *(Brian C.Rogers)*

(Below) US Air Force plans to name the Rockwell B-1B bomber "Excalibur" were reconsidered when it was brought to their attention that this was also the name of a popular brand of condom... long after entering service the B-1B became the "Lancer". *Nightmare* (86-0127) belongs to the 28th Bomb Squadron, part of the 384th Bomb Wing, and is seen in May 1992 at McConnell AFB near Wichita, Kansas. *(Jerry Geer)*

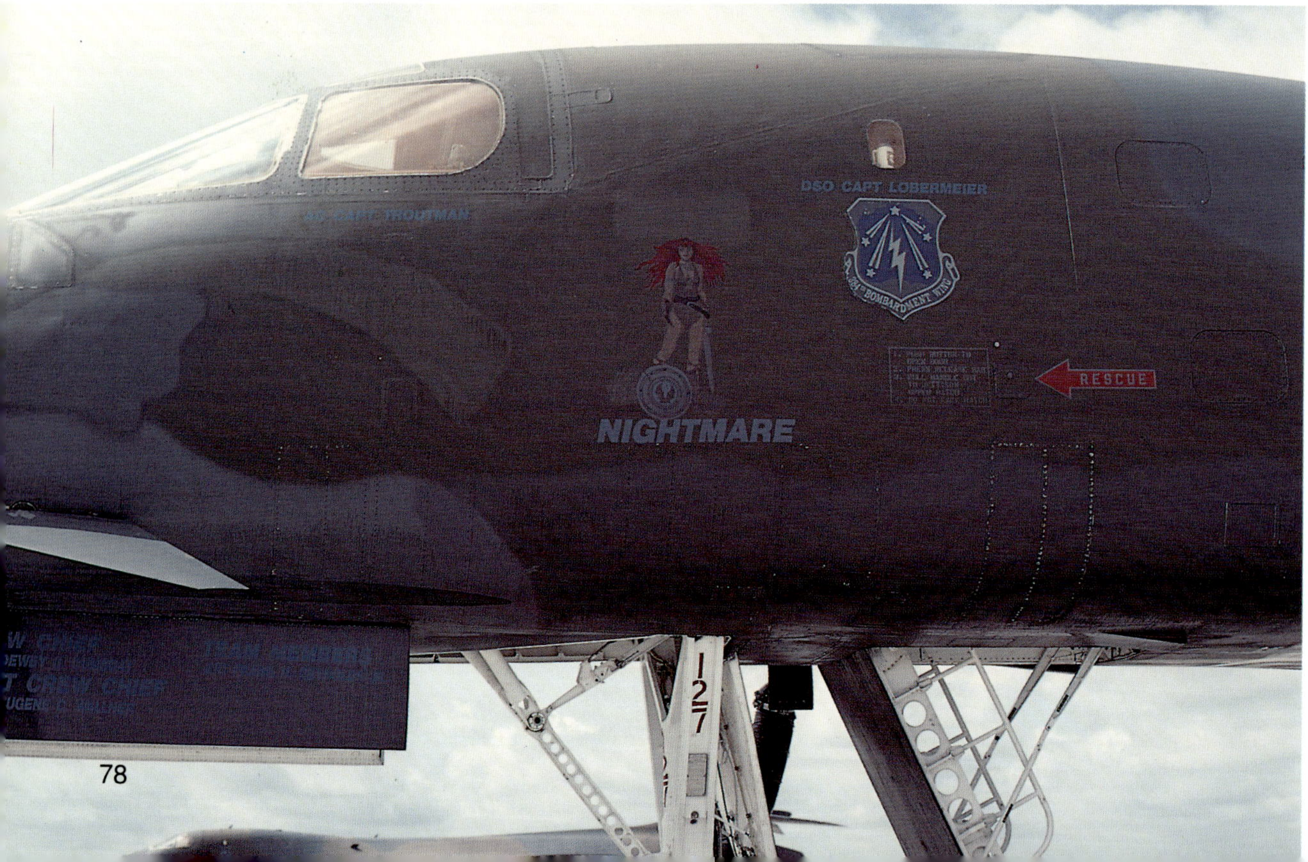

On 1 June 1992 most stateside fighters and bombers were subsumed into the newly created Air Combat Command. Air Force Chief of Staff Gen.Merrill McPeak used the phrase "global reach, global power" to describe his lean, mean fighting machine: "reach" being provided by Air Mobility Command's tankers and transports, "power" by ACC fighters and bombers. Unlike the mobility command, ACC adopted a rule that artwork could only appear on aircraft noses, thus killing off such unit distinctions as the Statue of Liberty which had previously appeared on the tails of B-52s. ACC spokesmen would not say whether they were adopting the same "gender neutral" policy for nose art as applied in the AMC; but it seems unlikely that the authorities will allow the creation of any new examples like *Lady of the Nite*, displayed here by a B-1B (85-0080) of the 28th Bomb Wing seen during a visit to Edwards AFB, California. *(Craig Kaston)*

Visiting Myrtle Beach, South Carolina from its home base at Dyess AFB, Texas, *Boss Hawg* is a B-1B (84-0051) of the 96th Bomb Wing; its relatively tasteful, if porcine nose art stands out nicely against the B-1B's "penetrator gray" paint scheme. Apart from the pig and the wing badge, note the "last four" of the aircraft's serial number painted vertically on the nose wheel leg. (The alert vehicle in the background also bears artwork and a callsign.) Virtually the entire B-1B fleet are adorned with nicknames and caricatures. *(Kevin Foy)*

Tails, Mostly

Fairchild A-10A Warthog (75-0307) of the 358th Fighter Squadron, 355th Fighter Wing at Davis-Monthan AFB, Arizona, in November 1990. The DM tail code comes from the base name; the insignia of the former Tactical Air Command is retained by the new Air Combat Command.
(Norman Taylor)

DM

AF 75 307

The USAF's Air Training Command (ATC) - scheduled to be renamed Air Training and Educational Command in 1994 - has long used graphic art to denote the wings and squadrons which create the service's pilots and other aircrew personnel. *Willie One* is a Northrop T-38A Talon (68-8217) of the 92nd Flying Training Squadron, 82nd Flying Training Wing, photographed at Williams AFB, Arizona, in November 1990. The base after which this Talon is named was among those selected to be closed in 1993. Note the ATC emblem, and the stylized serial number, on the gloss-white finish. *(Craig Kaston)*

Although the USAF has disbanded its "agressor" squadrons, F-16C Fighting Falcons from the 57th Fighter Wing at Nellis AFB, Nevada, provide a tactics cadre and fly as the "Red" force during Red Flag exercises. This F-16C (86-0271) wears the wing's WA tail code, taken from the term "Weapons Analysis" - a fair description of the 57th's wider mission - while ATD stands for "Air Tactics Development". The wing's distinctive checkerboard colors are displayed on the fintip. *(Craig Kaston)*

Lockheed TR-1A reconnaissance aircraft (80-1084) of the 9th Strategic Reconnaissance Wing at Beale AFB, California, in November 1990. In 1992 all TR-1As were redesignated U-2, reflecting their real identity as the final version of the famous spy plane dating from the 1950s. The wing's Maltese crosses and the dragon on the dead black fin give this unarmed aircraft a somewhat threatening air. *(Craig Kaston)*

SP is for Spangdahlem: this F-16C block 30 Fighting Falcon (86-0260) belongs to the 23rd Fighter Squadron, 52nd Fighter Wing at the German base. On 17 January 1993, fully two years after "Desert Storm", a virtually identical Falcon from this squadron (86-0262) shot down an Iraqi MiG-29 challenging the Allies' "no fly" sanctions above the 32nd Parallel. The artistic squadron logo on the fin is somewhat unusual. *(Norman Taylor)*

The North American OV-10A Bronco had, alas, been removed from the USAF inventory by the time this book went to press. In November 1990 this brightly plumed Bronco (67-14629) was the commander's aircraft for the 507th Tactical Air Control Wing at Shaw AFB, South Carolina - from which the tail code, seen here with the wing's designation, is derived. *(Norman Taylor)*

(Above) In 1993 the US Air Force reversed a longstanding plan and decided not to retire its fleet of F-4G Advanced Wild Weasels after all. The last warplanes remaining in service with the mission of attacking surface-to-air missile sites, their WW code is likely to remain part of the Air Force lexicon for the remainder of the century. A much-modified F-4E Phantom, this F-4G (69-0292) of the 562nd Tactical Fighter Squadron, 35th Tactical Fighter Wing is seen at George AFB, California, in November 1990. *(Craig Kaston)*

Its home base at Birmingham is presumably the origin of the BH tail code sported by this RF-4C Phantom II (65-0854) of the 106th Tactical Reconnaissance Squadron, Alabama ANG photographed in August 1991. The array of patches record all units which operated the RF-4C at that time. Alabama Guardsmen took RF-4Cs out to the Gulf during "Desert Shield", but the aircraft were taken over before the shooting started by Guardsmen from Reno, Nevada. *(Norman Taylor)*

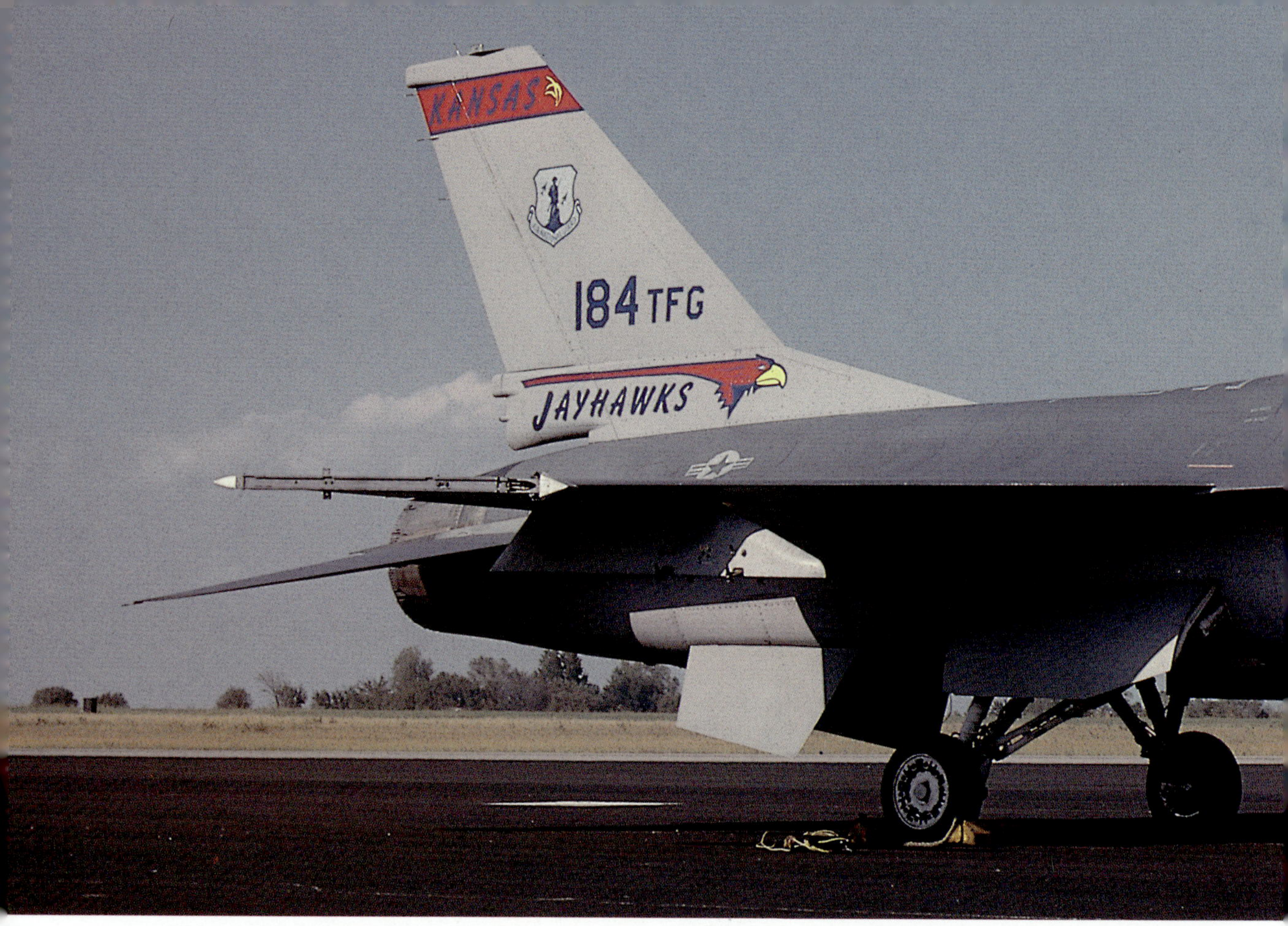
KANSAS
184 TFG
JAYHAWKS

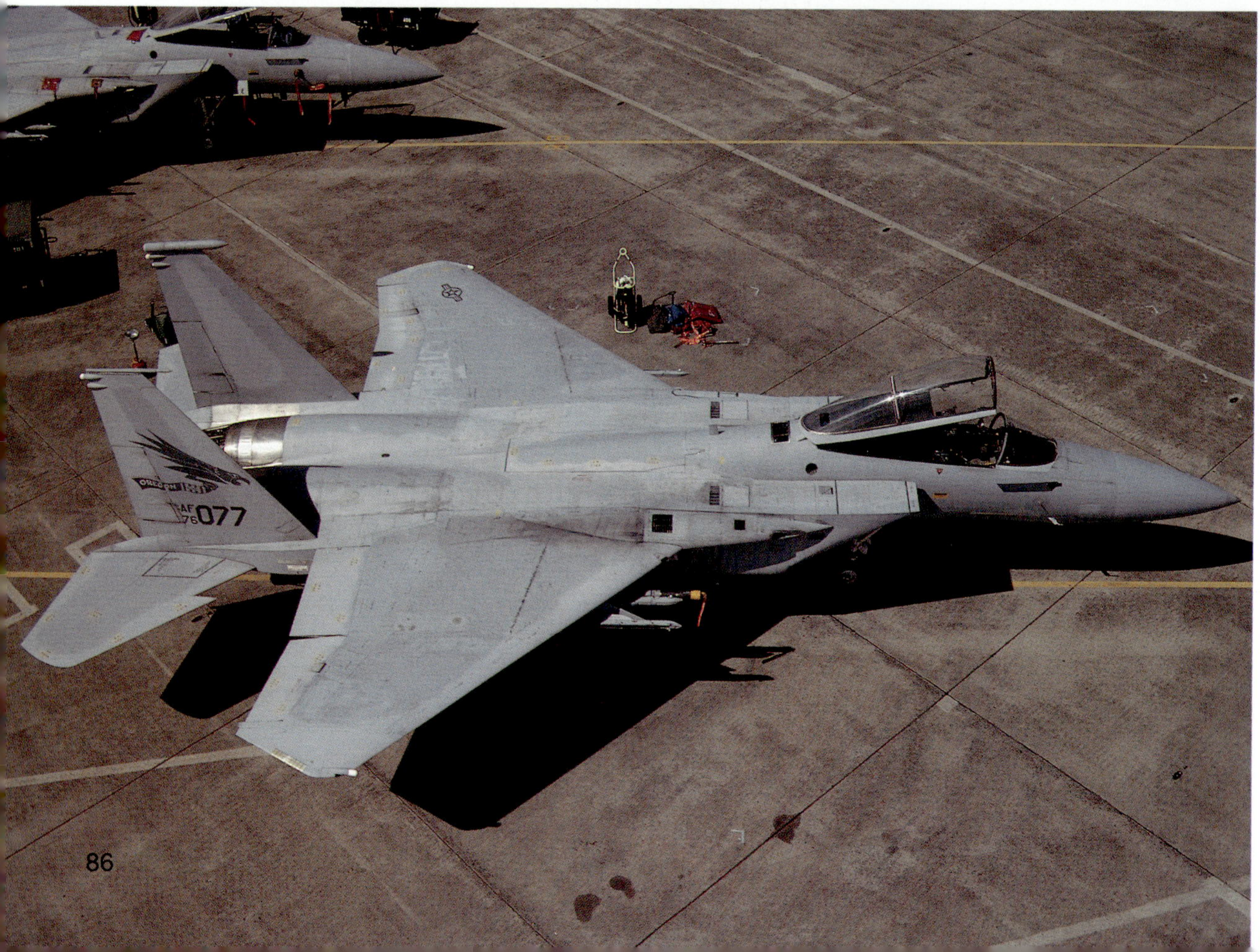
AF 76 077

(Left) McDonnell F-15A Eagle (76-0077) of the 123rd Fighter-Interceptor Squadron, Oregon ANG photographed in August 1990. *(Rene J.Francillon)*

(Above & below) The 127th Fighter Squadron, Kansas ANG, located at McConnell AFB at Wichita, is a Replacement Training Unit for the F-16 Fighting Falcon. The F-16A wears the colorful livery until recently sported by the "Jayhawks"; the F-16C (84-1297), photographed in June 1991, the austere grays of the latest toned-down scheme. *(Jerry Geer/ Norman Taylor)*

Local pride can still be shown in tones of gray: the tails of F-16C (84-1300) of the 163rd Tactical Fighter Squadron, Indiana ANG, at Shaw AFB, SC, in December 1991; and F-16A (81-0784) of the 186th Fighter-Interceptor Squadron, Montana ANG, at Great Falls in September 1990. *(Norman Taylor/Douglas Olson)*

The absence from these pages of the F-15E Strike Eagle is due solely to the fact that it has never worn distinctive nose art, even when the type was tweaking Saddam Hussein's nose in Operation "Desert Storm". The closest the Strike Eagle has come to gallery status is the wing commander's mount of the 4th Fighter Wing at Seymour Johnson AFB, North Carolina, where it was photographed in May 1991. F-15E (89-0499) bears the base's highlighted code, the commander's three-color fintip flash, the TAC emblem, and, on the inner surface, a subdued Eagle logo. *(Norman Taylor)*

(Left) The 480th and 81st are two of the fighter squadrons assigned to the 52nd Fighter Wing at Spangdahlem, Germany; they are represented here by F-16C block 30 Fighting Falcons bearing their tail insignia - respectively (86-0224) with a red and (86-0230) with a yellow stripe. *(Norman Taylor)*

(Right) The new Air Force Materiel Command, created on 1 July 1992, handles test and logistics operations, including the fabled flight test center at Edwards AFB, California. AFMC says its job is "integrated weapons systems management from cradle to grave"; and since it has a number of "one of a kind" airplanes it is still possible to find AFMC flying machines adorned with unique logos and colors. This is the AFTI/CAS F-16A Fighting Falcon (75-0750), a test ship for Advanced Fighter Technology/Close Air Support duties. Originally an early developmental aircraft in the F-16 series, it is now used to evaluate new flight control systems as well as new ways of achieving precision in air-to-ground ordnance delivery. *(Craig Kaston)*

(Right) Retired from service early in the 1990s, the USAF's extraordinary Lockheed SR-71A Blackbird was given a designation in sequence with bombers (following the XB-70A), perhaps in part to veil its intelligence-gathering mission. This SR-71A (64-17960) wearing its "nose" art on the tail seems to be called *Jaws II.* Individualized artwork on the Blackbird was extremely unusual; for much of its career the renowned spy plane flew in a dead black finish with red serials. *(Craig Kaston)*

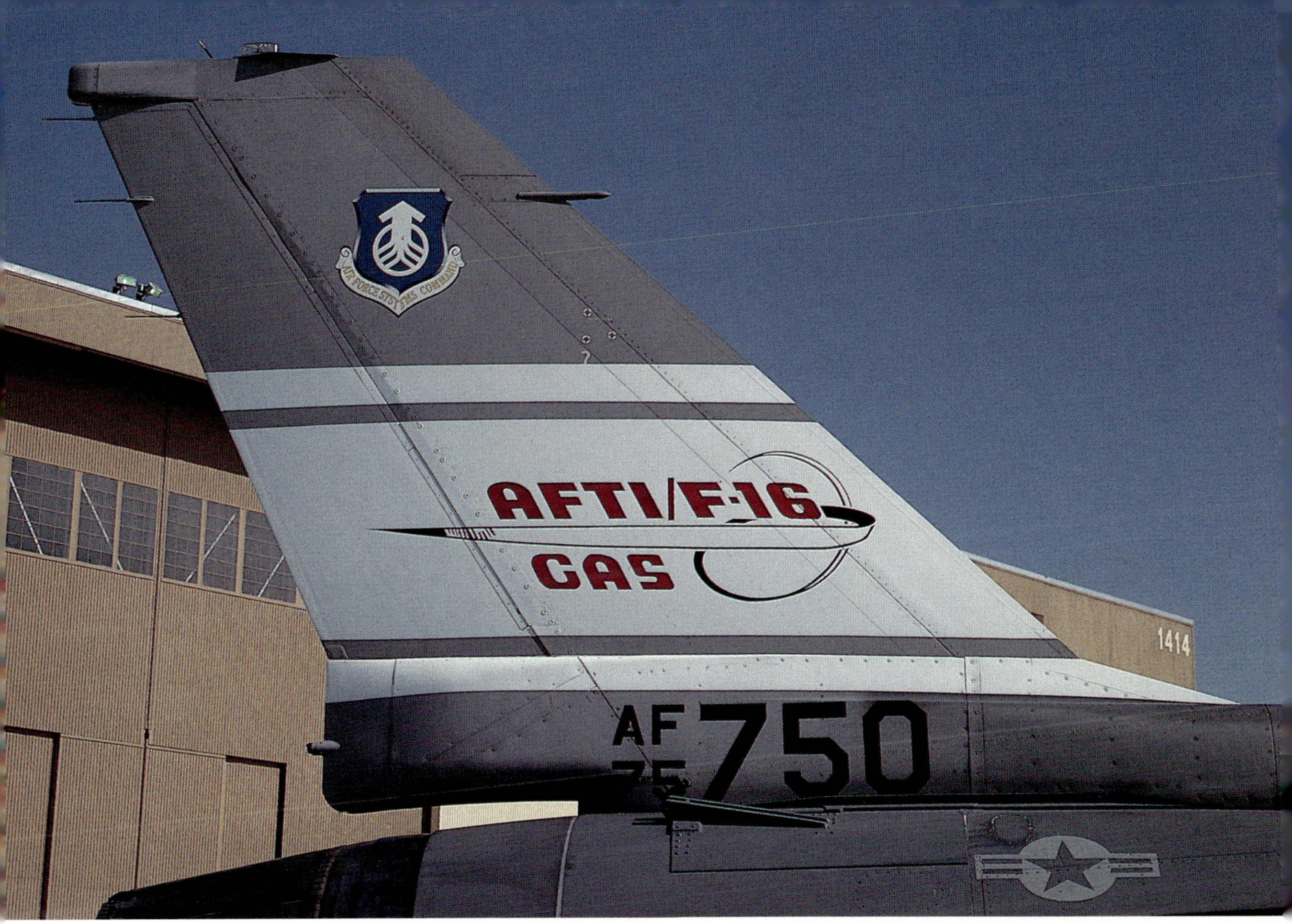
AIR FORCE SYSTEMS COMMAND
AFTI/F-16
GAS
AF
75
750
1414

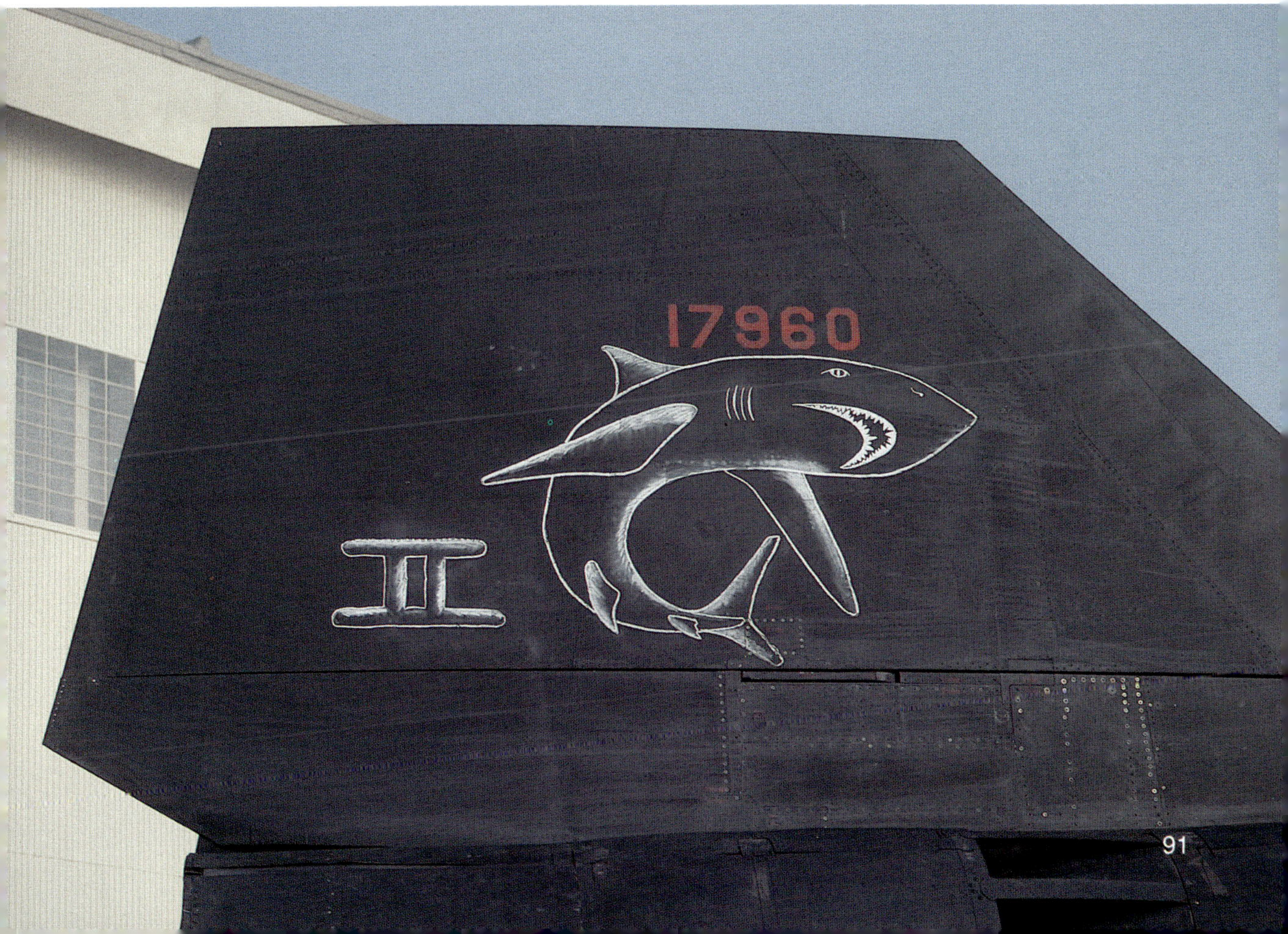
17960

The Big Finish

How better to round off this stroll through the gallery of warplane art than with the highest-scoring fighter of Operation "Desert Storm"? The 33rd Tactical Fighter Wing (58th and 60th TFS) from Eglin AFB, Florida, racked up most of the few air-to-air victories which Saddam's bunker-loving air force gave the Allies any opportunity to achieve; and McDonnell F-15C Eagle (85-0102) *Gulf Spirit* was the top-scoring fighter of the bunch, with three kills. Photographed on 29 August 1991 as the wing commander's aircraft, it has his three-color stripes on the outside fintips above the Eglin tail code and wing designation, and an Eagle motif on the black inner fin bands. Unusually, matching artwork is applied to both sides of the nose. *(Norman Taylor)*

Two alternative displays of kill markings on the port side of 85-0102. *Gulf Spirit* refers not to the Persian Gulf, but the Gulf of Mexico, and the F-15C carries an outline of the state of Florida with a blue star marking Eglin AFB. When photographed by Robert F.Dorr in June 1991 the F-15C bore three Iraqi tricolor flags denoting total kills by pilots flying this aircraft; plus a single green star for the one of these three scored by 0102's normally assigned pilot, Col.Rick Parsons.

By the time Norman Taylor took his shot on 29 August 1991 the plane was assigned to Col."Speedy" Martin, and the kill tally had changed to three green stars marked in white for a MiG-23 between two Su-22s. The three light-colored rectangles beneath the map are formation-keeping "slime lights", so called from the putrid green color they emit when in use.

Col. Rick Parsons
GULF
SPIRIT
PULL "T" HANDLE
EXTEND CABLE 8 FT.
PULL TO JETTISON
CANOPY
RESCUE

Also available in this series:

Wings 1:	'F-15E Strike Eagle' by Hans Halberstadt	
Wings 2:	'US Navy: West Coast Warriors' by George Hall	
Wings 3:	'California High: Warbirds of the West Coast' by Michael O'Leary	
Wings 4:	'F-111 Aardvark' by Hans Halberstadt	
Wings 5:	'Marine Muscle: Hornet & Harrier' by Hans Halberstadt	
Wings 6:	'Rhino: The Immortal Phantom II' by Joe Cupido	